Map of the Alpes-Maritimes département - Côte d'Azur (French Riviera) - France

PAYSAGES D'AZUR

The sea, mountains and heritage of the Côte d'Azur

JACQUES BRUYAS

PAYSAGES D'AZUR

The sea, mountains and heritage of the Côte d'Azur

Foreword by DIDIER VAN CAUWELAERT

ÉDITIONS GILLETTA

THE HINTERLAND. "Home is not where you stay, but the place you return to" in Montherlant's words. Growing up in Nice, for the child I had been, the teenager I was and the man I hoped to become, meant above all being able to leave Nice and return later with new insight, renewed pleasure: the hindsight and distance from that parallel world in my eyes, the hinterland.

The road up the lower Var valley offers a deceptive promise of linear infinity and escape to an American-style world, an illusion soon dissipated in narrowing gorges, hairpin turns and their retching, a gateway to adventure, different landscapes, mirages, secrets buried in the hollow of the weekend. My first village in the Vésubie valley: a name long forgotten though I well remember both its setting and atmosphere.

I was six years old. We were visiting one of my parents' friends who, I had been warned, led a "double life" two days a week. Consequently, we had to avoid any allusions to Nice so as not to hurt our hostess's feelings. This was a disconcertingly perilous way of causing gaffes in spite of all our intentions of avoiding them. When the lady of the house asked me where I went to school, I answered: "Clermont-Ferrand". The name of this city in central France came to me spontaneously. Beyond a mark of my discretion, the name represented the ultimate in exoticism for me, probably because of its resemblance with *"maréchal-ferrant"* (blacksmith in French), a trade straight out of the myth of the American West weighing on my mind at the time. Soon it would give way to the mysteries of the yellow stone *mas* that harboured a "double life" at the bottom of a garden among the loose rocks planted with tiny signs bearing the names of the invisible flowers whose seeds had been sown there. The association, in my head at least, of the notion of hinterland and double life would enjoy a great future.

Later, we were involved in a piece of land at the foot of the village of Gattières, where we spent our Sundays in a virtual holiday home, whose location, style and orientation changed every week. We took measurements, drew plans, built castles in the air. "Here is your bedroom, there, you will store your bike and your Ping-Pong table in winter..." I agreed. It was so strange to watch the games of grownups. Picnicking in the tall grass, they opened doors, walked along partitions and admired the view from imaginary windows. Periodically, I brought them back to their senses. I did not want them to build a house there: they would have destroyed a splendid oak tree they had no right to cut down. Docile and conciliatory, they would move elsewhere. But I always found a new tree that needed protection from the dreams of adults, and the threat of bulldozers. In the end, our house in Gattières never materialised. Or rather, we had ten, twenty, a hundred: all possible houses. They still haunt the site, even though today, to the uninitiated, the land, long since sold, may reveal no more than a housing development of rendered breeze blocks separated by hedges of thujas in place of the oaks my obstinacy had saved for a time.

Back in Nice, the rest of the week meant school, the beach, the real world, sunburns and fist fights. My typically Flemish physiognomy, my unpronounceable outlandish name and the mockery they inspired, the schoolyard brawls during recreation... They were all like a trailer for a "normal" existence in which, because of stupidity and majority rule, being different becomes a matter of solitude, a paradoxical gift we learn to appreciate only much later, when the majority are reduced to playing the role of extras.

In the hinterland, my own double life continued. With my motorbike, I had a fiancée in every village: the girl sitting on the edge of the fountain away from the others, seeking escape in her reflection or dreaming of her Prince Charming without realising I was the one she awaited. Obviously, she would not always be happy; I would make her suffer since she would not be alone in my heart and perhaps some day she would drown herself in the fountain out of despair... Then I would leave, magnanimously, for another village, another drama of life and love. At the age of thirteen, my relations with girls could be likened to those I entertained with trees: I built nothing, but I undertook a great deal of preservation.

Fortunately, there was the theatre. As part of an amateur group inspired by the desire to convey cultural benefits to remote places, I experienced the blue van and covered caravan, the stage set up at dawn on the village square, dressing rooms improvised in people's homes, in the grocery or bakery, with the last rehearsal whispered to the rustle of the bead curtains, putting on makeup on crates of lemonade, in the midst of the smell of fruit or the heat of the baker's oven, the polite perplexity of the audience of villagers whom we were initiating to Brecht's expressionism, Sartre's existentialism or Kafka's denunciation of urban life. Mortified by the incongruous laughter triggered by our performance, we decided one day to put ourselves on a level with our audience by including plays in Nissart dialect in our repertory. No one was ever able to understand us. We declaimed their ancestral memory in the Nissart language of Francis Gag and André Compan, which differed from the "mountain" dialect. Our arrival in the village of Saint-Étienne-de-Tinée one morning was greeted with cries of *"V'la les Z'Hollandais!"* (The Dutchmen are here).

The more trouble we had communicating our message, the more our audience grew in size and the more they seemed to enjoy watching us. Those moments of mysterious complicity at the heart of the misunderstanding left profound traces in me. There is always a resonance in sincerity, an echo stronger than the barrier of roots and language, that needs no analysis as long as the magic lasts. Whether we came to deliver a hermetic message or stir up some unknown memory, whether we came as attentive ethnographers or narrow-minded cultural colonists, it was the passion alone that counted, the determination to reach out to others, to talk or understand, since only people can take you elsewhere, change you and reveal to you through their empathy or lack of comprehension, curiosity, tolerance and openness.

The hinterland of Nice is the best antidote for preconceived ideas and the ready-made images that too often sum up Nice, its climate, gangsters, retired folk, Promenade des Anglais... I could have evoked landscapes, scents, customs, the realities of yore. What my pen writes without my intervention is exactly the opposite. It is that share of collective subconscious sensed by the imagination at various times in life, fashioning it better, perhaps, than the meticulous upkeep of its roots. Does my dream house in Gattières have any less existence than the home in the forest of Rambouillet in which I am writing these words? Was it harder to communicate with my very first readers, apparently unfamiliar with the world in which I wished to take them, than with those who praise or reject me today, believing, in both cases, that they perceive my intentions and know me? Was I born in Nice or in the double lives inspired to me by the hinterland?

Leaving behind me the villages, back down to the lower Var and Paillon valleys from the slopes of Mont-Bego to return to the rites, customs and language of the real world, I remember that my love of Nice was different. My town had become the home described by Montherlant: a port where I could relax between two crossings, a stopover in a familiar regulated world, where I could "inspect myself", restock my reason before casting off again on the road to dreams... a port open on the hinterland.

Didier van Cauwelaert

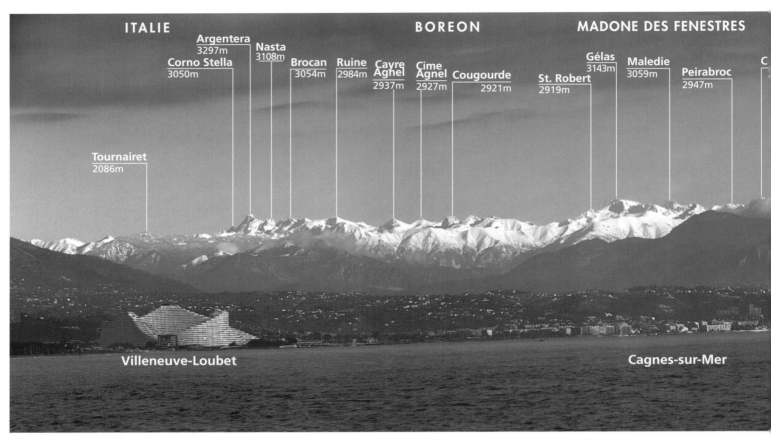

ITALIE   BOREON   MADONE DES FENESTRES

Argentera
3297m

Nasta
3108m

Corno Stella
3050m

Brocan
3054m

Ruine
2984m

Cayre
Agnel
2937m

Cime
Agnel
2927m

Cougourde
2921m

St. Robert
2919m

Gélas
3143m

Maledie
3059m

Peirabroc
2947m

Tournairet
2086m

Villeneuve-Loubet   Cagnes-sur-Mer

The highest peaks of the Alpes-Maritimes, seen from the city of Antibes in winter (Photograph by Claude Raybaud).

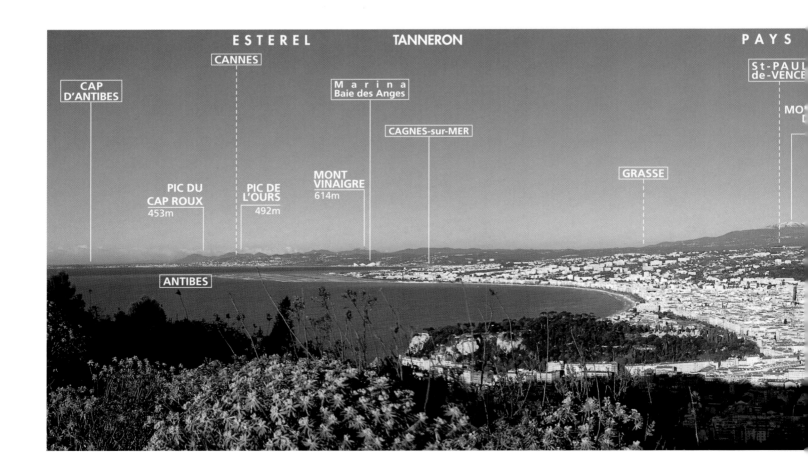

ESTEREL   TANNERON   PAYS

CANNES

CAP
D'ANTIBES

Marina
Baie des Anges

CAGNES-sur-MER

St-PAUL
de-VENCE

MO

PIC DU
CAP ROUX
453m

PIC DE
L'OURS
492m

MONT
VINAIGRE
614m

GRASSE

ANTIBES

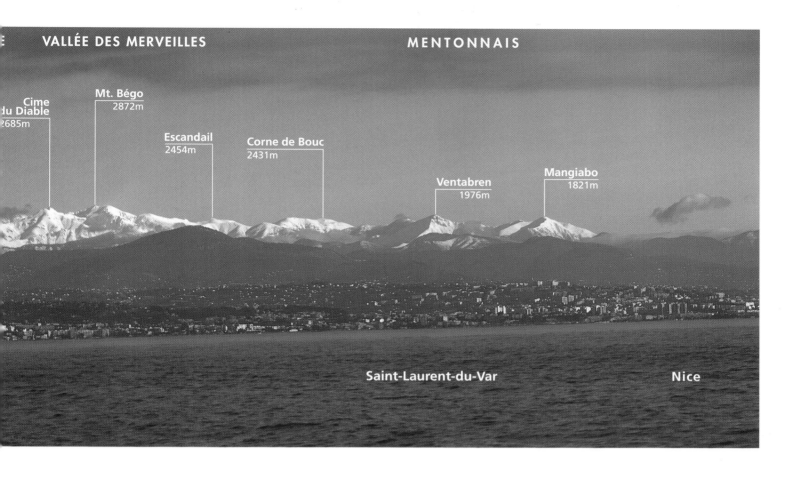

VALLÉE DES MERVEILLES   MENTONNAIS

Cime
du Diable
2685m

Mt. Bégo
2872m

Escandail
2454m

Corne de Bouc
2431m

Ventabren
1976m

Mangiabo
1821m

Saint-Laurent-du-Var   Nice

The City of Nice and the Pre-Alps of Grasse, seen from the Mont-Alban on a spring morning (Photograph by Claude Raybaud).

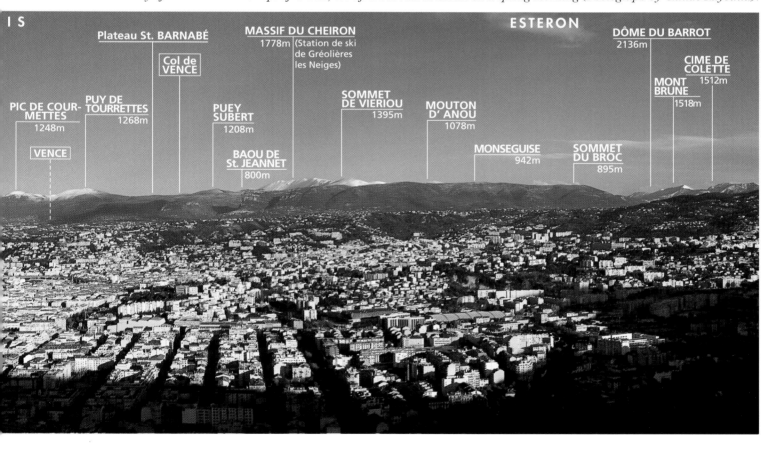

I S   ESTERON

Plateau St. BARNABÉ

MASSIF DU CHEIRON
1778m (Station de ski
de Gréolières
les Neiges)

DÔME DU BARROT
2136m

Col de
VENCE

CIME DE
COLETTE
1512m

PIC DE COUR-
METTES
1248m

PUY DE
TOURRETTES
1268m

PUEY
SUBERT
1208m

SOMMET
DE VIERIOU
1395m

MOUTON
D' ANOU
1078m

MONT
BRUNE
1518m

VENCE

BAOU DE
St. JEANNET
800m

MONSEGUISE
942m

SOMMET
DU BROC
895m

ALPES-MARITIMES:
a wedding of Sea and Earth

Alpes-Maritimes, maritime Alps: the meaning is clear, imposed from the beginning of our Era by the legions marching into Gaul. Eighteen centuries later, the Roman Provincia has left its signature, which France would retain. Provence and the Comté de Nice moved closer together, but sealing their union, the Alps remained "maritime". Nature reigns supreme in making this land the quintessence of contrasts. Geology, climate, flora, human history; nothing here is simple or predictable. In a few tens of kilometres, the highest peaks tower at altitudes in excess of 3,000 metres above sea level, before plunging, after pausing briefly on the beaches of pebbles or sand, into transparent abysses. Transported by the view from the coastline, an early geographer compared the majestic mountain amphitheatre to "an agitated sea whose waves are suddenly solidified." The physical geography of the Alpes-Maritimes expresses a mythological allegory: the goddess Earth surging forth from the waters. The wedding of Sea and Earth, begun at the dawn of time, left marine fossils on the greatest heights, carved splendid natural architecture, engendered scrubby vegetation, dictated the exceptional perched settlement patterns and rich sacred geography. The Alpes-Maritimes département is a chaos of plateaux and inclines, slopes and gorges. At the bottom, countless capricious torrents wind their way, or churn, fed by the sudden cloudbursts that alternate with endless azure skies. We all know how the special light here charmed painters, which explains the prominence of art museums. Nowhere else on the Mediterranean coast is there such a juxtaposition of a tropical environment on the coast and glacial phenomena inland, prized by athletes, in so strikingly short a distance. Preserved from monotony,

with extraordinarily rich fauna, the Alpes-Maritimes have been peopled since the dawn of Prehistoric time, as attested by spectacular caves (Lazaret), open sites (Terra Amata) and under the stars in the Mercantour mountains (Vallée des Merveilles). Protecting themselves against the danger from the sea, which brought in Greek and Roman builders and colonisers, the native peoples, Ligurians and Celts, lived relatively autonomously, in conditions as harsh as their mountains, without, however, being able to escape from the ebb and flow of European history. Perhaps for having crossed it too quickly, that same Europe chose, two centuries ago, to return here, to make it a resort. After being closed to the world, this land suddenly found itself at its centre, the rendezvous and playground for crowned heads and celebrities. Tourism, which makes this one of its most prestigious destinations today with several million visitors annually, opened the ball, and since then it has never ceased. It is something exhilarating. Fortunately, the Alpes-Maritimes was inspired by ancestral wisdom and made the best of the modern infrastructures required for such activity (airport, banking system). Thus, a complement was found for its young qualified population by stimulating such activities as research and production, attracting foreign laboratories and managerial centres in state-of-the-art technologies: telecommunications, life, earth and environmental sciences. In the past, the quality of life was taken for granted. Today it is something to be constantly reclaimed. The great challenge for the future facing the Alpes-Maritimes, its coastline, villages and valleys, will be to maintain its plurality for the greatest satisfaction of its people and its visitors.

C O N T E N T S

The legend of the Riviera! In 1760, Tobias Smollett came to Nice because of its reputedly wholesome climate. He strolled through landscapes whose rustic simplicity is known to us thanks to contemporary engravings. On foot and on horseback, he scoured the paths between the fishing and farming villages scattered in the hills. He strode along the coast dotted with tamarisk, oak and oleander, interspersed with lagoons towards Antibes and Cannes. He ventured to the solitude of Èze and Monaco on the fearsome mule trails overhanging the coastline where the mountain abruptly fall into the sea. But the Scottish writer would certainly never have imagined that one day the call of seagulls would be covered by the roar of "cabin cruisers" carrying the stars of cinema and television famous on all five continents. That sumptuous villas and hotels nestled among the rocks and pine trees would host unforgettable receptions for the international jet set. That great commercial centres and bustling seaside resorts would form a 115-kilometre stretch along the coast. That the neon signs of the casinos and the lights of luxury yachts anchored in a dozen harbours would be reflected in the same waters. That businessmen and scientists would gather in great international conventions, or the finest athletes in major meets with names evocative of Antiquity, Nikaïa or Herculis. Yet Tobias Smollett did have a part in this metamorphosis thanks to his Book of Travels that inaugurated the international promotion of what another visitor, a Frenchman, would qualify a century later as the *"Côte d'Azur"*. He was one of the instigators of the first British colony that settled in Nice. Before the discovery of Cannes, by another influential figure from the British Isles, prevented from reaching the Comté de Nice because of a cholera epidemic. Menton's celebrity was also of medical origin. But the seers stood watch over such calamitous auspices: the thousands of young consumptives who flocked here to breathe their last hope in the warm sunlight did not come alone. Leaving the wintry cold of the North by the month of October, the crowned heads of Europe came, too, with statesmen, financiers, merchants in their wake, as well as "fortune hunters, courtesans, gold-diggers, swindlers of all sorts." Within a few months (but what months!), the tranquil land between "Cannes where one poses" and "Monte Carlo where one gambles" changed into a frivolous bustling Babel, rife with festivities and entertainment, whimsical or spicy anecdotes. This was where artistic reputations were made, where the first great industrialists displayed inventions that were sometimes completely mad, where grandiose homes, some very strange, rose out of the ground. "They are certainly Englishmen, although I can't say if they're French or German," Alexandre Dumas heard the natives say. The tragic hiccups of history and the vicissitudes of fashion dispersed little of this carefree life, so well portrayed in Raoul Dufy's works. It was not until the period between the two World Wars that the diaphanous creatures with their parasols gave way to other incarnations. Women became the symbol of a wild time of speed and pretence, with which the Riviera became intoxicated between the asphalt and the surf. With an aura of luxury, these increasingly denuded Vestals would inspire perfumers, couturiers, decorators, writers and painters of a modernity-to-be so well captured in black and white by Jacques Henri Lartigue's camera. They also began to spread languidly on glossy magazine covers, ambassadresses of the now legendary Riviera, a legend that persists to this day. A fragrance of refinement and sensuality that Coco Chanel, who had sought refuge on the coast to forget a heartbreak, immortalised in her "N° 5", with which Marilyn Monroe decked her nights.

HE SHORES OF THE RIVIERA

The sea, mountains and heritage of the Côte d'Azur

CANNES AND ITS VICINITY: the Star

Of all the cities studding the coast like a foam-rimmed diadem, the very name of Cannes exhales the headiest fragrance of all. Looking into the eyes of the women pronouncing the name, the novelist Paul Morand could see a "costly gleam": the ransom for the sheer pleasure of quality. Luxury and voluptuousness have been linked, for over a century, with this city of stars that Guy de Maupassant, a connoisseur of ladies, compared to a "woman lying in a semi-circle". Crowning her head, the old town surmounted with its dismantled belfry: the entire past of a modest fishing village surrounded by marshes and living in the ecclesiastical orbit of the Isles of Lérins. Provençal volubility pervades the narrow aisles of the Forville market and the little streets on either side of

1 *Le Suquet, the historic centre of Cannes, from the remains of the 14th-century castle overlooking the bay and the old harbour. Today, the fishing nets that used to pile up there until the early 20th century are replaced with splendid yachts alongside the traditional "pointus" moored in the heart of the city.*

2 *The mimosa tree, related to the acacia family, came originally from Australia. It grows only in non-limestone soil. Early in the year, the flowers are picked for perfumery and to be shipped as fresh cut flowers all over the world.*

3 *The Tanneron. This crystalline mountain range has very specific vegetation: eucalyptus and mimosa, wild and cultivated. From the highest point, the view stretches over the entire massif all the way to the sea.*

1 *Château de la Napoule. This 14th-century fortress was purchased by the American sculptor Henry Clews in 1918. He had it restored and asked stone cutters to carve his satirical creations over the entire castle, open with its gardens to visitors in the afternoon. The H. Clews Foundation provides accommodation for resident artists from the world over and organises various artistic events.*

Rue Meynadier. From the shoulders to the feet of this poeticised feminine body, La Croisette unfurls a gleaming drapery of flowers and chrome. In the immaculate white façades and overly ornate architecture of luxury hotels with magical names (Carlton, Majestic, Martinez, Miramar), all the world's stars have, at least once, been mirrored under the admiring gaze of the young jet set or in front of the cold blinking eye of the cameras. When holidaymakers play in the wavelets under the burning sun, lavish serenity seeks refuge in the fresh gardens or shaded terraces of the sumptuous villas nestled in the hills of La Croix-des-Gardes and La Californie. Successive waves of cosmopolitan occupants have confirmed Lord Brougham's choice.

2 *The Forest of Pointe de l'Aiguille Park is a protected coastal stretch covering 7 hectares in the Estérel massif, starting from Théoule via Promenade André-Pradayrol. Trails lead to small inlets and the rocks of Pointe de l'Aiguille.*

Further up, Le Cannet is not the creation of holiday visitors; this town never aimed to become an annexe for its opulent neighbour. At the foot of the crystalline hills, with their red glow like an iron portal in the setting sun, from which emerge trainfuls of wide-eyed stares, Théoule is the gateway to a paradise fragrant with the mimosas in the Tanneron range. The castle on the shore of La Napoule has lost all its defensive stance. In spite of its bellicose ancestry, it was imaginatively restored by a very rich American and now forms a foundation for young artists. The golf course between Mandelieu and Cannes is a dream of England created by a Tsarist Grand Duke, where the greens, still smelling of the sea, defy the umbrella pines

1 *The Festival Hall of Cannes, built in 1982 at the Western end of La Croisette, hosts many artistic and professional events: the International Film Festival, as well as theatre, ballet, concerts, MIDEM, MIP-TV... The building offers a wide range of facilities for these many different events and houses a Casino in its West wing.*

2 *From the very start, Hôtel Majestic, built in 1926 by the architect Théo Petit, was considered to be one of the best equipped luxury hotels in the region. The hotel was renovated in 1980, in the Art-Deco style that has always characterised it.*

3 *The Bay of Cannes from a beach on La Croisette.*

4 *"In the immaculate white façades and overly ornate architecture of luxury hotels with magical names: the Carlton..." built in 1911 by the architect Charles Delmas, has 355 rooms and suites.*

and the Siagne River. This quiet stream has given its name to the green valley with its many small farms. Up to the village of Auribeau, the ruins of water mills recall that rowing was not originally its sole vocation. Huddled around its virtual ramparts, of which only the so-called "Saracen" gate remains, Mougins resembles a snail, still dormant in the warm air, its horns materialised by the mediaeval castle and the Romanesque church, though this image in itself does not explain why the village has become a Mecca for haute cuisine. Studding the sea like two water lilies just off the coast, the Isles of Lérins were probably a spiritual centre long before Christianity. The fortified monastery is one of the region's rare examples of 11th-century military and religious architecture.

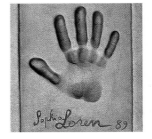

Minelli, Clément, Lean, Clouzot, Saura, Bresson, Welles, Fellini, Tati, Buñuel, Altman, Reed, Losey, Herzog, Kurosawa, Coppola, Schloendorff, Truffaut, Tarkovski... Although they owe none of their talent to the International Film Festival, they do owe it some of their recognition. And, consequently, it has served to build the incomparable renown those film directors, whose names, randomly selected here, stud the firmament of the world of motion pictures. This is the very nature of the Cannes Festival, born just as the light of peace was about to go out in the Second World War. Then, it was revived in the middle of the century, which it has traversed, accompanied by all the glitter, scandal, clichés and unforgettable smiles of the likes of Schneider, Loren, Bardot, Hayworth, Davis, Adjani, Mangano, Bergman, Stone... Viewing the films deemed most representative of the year to reward their makers and actors, the cinema gathers every year in May, behind a panel made up of actors, writers and musicians, to revel in "a fortnight of elsewhere, a fortnight of dreams, a fortnight in which fiction replaces reality." Cannes becomes the Babylon of film with the touch of Midas, Pygmalion, demiurges and their creatures, towards whom converge the lenses of hundreds of photographers and journalists and the entire world's star-struck eyes.

1 *The grand staircase to the Festival Hall during the Film Festival: "Cannes becomes the Babylon of film..."*

2 *Sharon Stone climbing the steps to the Festival Hall.*

3 *In 1850, the authorities of Cannes decided to create a Boulevard along the Bay to satisfy the city's rich winter visitors. Boulevard de la Croisette was inaugurated in 1870. Stretching in a curving line along the waterfront, it separates the luxury hotels, or* palaces, *from the beaches.*

The Isles of Lérins give Cannes a necessary touch of mystery and mysticism. This begins with the geography and history of the two largest islands, so different yet so complementary in size: one virtually a wilderness, the other farmed; one a military stronghold, the other a religious haven. From the beginning of time, they have been distinguished, one masculine, the other feminine, as exemplified by the legend of the monk Honorat and Marguerite, his spiritual sister. The legend of the almond tree, blooming several times a year, adds an aura of fantasy to the story of the first evangelisers of Provence, who made even Attila the Hun relent. Today's Cistercian abbey, not open to visitors, except for the museum and church, and no longer that of its saintly founder, is a splendid place to see from the outside as you head for the fortified monastery. To the North, it stands as a counterpart to the Royal Fort whose impressive bastions guard famous secrets. Who was the "Man in the Iron Mask", and why was he locked up in the fort on Sainte-Marguerite? How did Maréchal Bazaine escape with the help of the woman he loved? And you cannot expect your mind to be cleared by the vapours of Lérina, *the liqueur concocted from wine by the silent monks.*

Saint Honorat belongs to a community of Cistercian monks who grow vine and lavender. They continue to live in strict observance of the Rule of Saint Benedict (requiring a rigorous balance between the spiritual life and physical activity).
The present church, built in 1875 and designed by Viollet-le-Duc, and the museum are open to the public.

The Isles of Lérins, Sainte-Marguerite and Saint-Honorat, are located to the Southwest of La Croisette and offer a unique excursion on the coast of the Alpes-Maritimes. The two islands are separated by Passage du Frioul, a popular mooring for yachtsmen.

1 *The Mandelieu golf course was founded in 1891 by Grand Duke Michael of Russia. It is one of the finest golf courses of the time, in a natural setting of umbrella pine forest and streams.*

2 *Étang de Fontmerle. A splendid protected pond, covering 5 hectares on the edge of La Valmasque park.*

3 *Notre-Dame-de-Vie, a chapel for a local pilgrimage since the 12th century.*

4 *Mougins.* The name Mons Ægitna *first appears in the 8th century in the Countship of Antibes. It is typical of the mediaeval Provençal villages, its houses spiralling around the castle and surrounded by a rampart.It has long been popular with modern and contemporary artists (including Picasso, Picabia...).*

5 *"Mougins resembles a snail, still dormant in the warm air..."*

GRASSE AND ITS VICINITY:
capital of the poetic industry

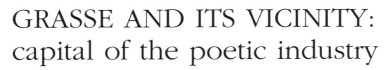

Grasse collects qualifying epithets and willingly accepts those of "wholesome" and "Provençal". Its episcopal complex (cathedral, clock tower and bishop's palace, now the Town Hall) is justly qualified as exceptional. Its old aristocratic families are prestigious, some going as far afield as the Americas in search of glory. Some of these memories are recalled in Amiral de Grasse's château in Le Bar-sur-Loup. And there is one title the town proudly vindicates: that of perfume capital of the world. Each town on the coast can boast a share in the reputation of excellence in the area of tourism. Grasse claims to have been the cradle and still be the heart of the "only poetic industry". From here, the sea is in full view, but under

[1] Place aux Aires *was created in the 14th century, a threshing floor for grain. Fullers also washed hides in basins filled with running water from a canal crossing the entire length of the square. Today, lined with 17th and 18th-century houses and arcades, it hosts the fruit and vegetable market in the morning.*

[2] *Flowers still inspire events in Grasse. With* Exporose *in May, the Jasmine Festival in August, horticulturists from the world over come here to display their production.*

[3] *Grasse has the remains of human occupation going far back in prehistory. In the 10th century, the rocky promontory provided refuge for the people fleeing the Saracens. Ca. 1300, the town surrounded itself with a rampart wall, inside which the houses stood several storeys tall, lining dark narrow streets and tiny squares. In the early 18th century, splendid private homes were built outside the wall and surrounded by fine gardens.*

*T*he industry of scents. Those distilleries that have not been torn down have become museums with sparkling copper pieces mirroring visitors' faces. Irises are brought in from Tuscany, vanilla from Madagascar, cinnamon from the island of Mayotte, orange blossoms from Tunisia, while roses and even jasmine are emigrating to other climes. Heavy and fine chemistry centres have also moved elsewhere. Grasse remains unique, however, because it has maintained its industrial potential. With powerful enterprises, some listed on the Stock Exchange with hundreds of millions of francs in sales, and a myriad of small inventive companies sprouting everywhere, the city remains amazingly dynamic. With more than half the French production capacity in essential oils, natural raw materials for perfumery and natural and synthetic flavours, it represents 6% of the market worldwide. It also enjoys unique, irreplaceable capital in terms of know-how: 80% of "jus" for perfumes are created by specialised "noses" in Grasse, who are able to devise new fragrances and, especially, know how to create them. Although gloves sacrificed perfume to synthetic substances, they have been largely replaced by prepared foods, detergents, beverages, soaps, pastries, insecticides, sweets, ice creams...

"Grasse enjoys unique, irreplaceable capital in terms of know-how: 80% of jus *for perfumes are created by specialised 'noses' able to devise new fragrances."* Perfumery, first linked to the leather-tanning industry in the 13th century, began developing in 1700 thanks to the popularity of scented leather goods.
The microclimate here is ideal for growing the most delicate flowers: rose, jasmine, jonquil, narcissus, carnation, orange blossom... Today, the factories are turning towards new markets, flavouring, etc.

1 *Saint-Laurent church in Magagnosc was built in the 15th century, its Baroque façade in the 18th century and its bell tower topped by a fine campanile in the 19th century.*

① Originally built in
the 12th century, the
Romanesque church of
Saint-Trophyme in Opio
was renovated in
the 15th century.

② Gourdon is a fortified
mediaeval village with a
panoramic view extending
over 80 km of coastline.
Around the castle, the
three tiers of terraced
gardens, planted with
orange trees, are designed
in the style of Le Nôtre.
The castle, originally built in
the 11th century, and said to
be of Saracen origin, became
a stronghold for the Counts
of Provence in 1200, and
was rebuilt in 1610, by
Louis de Lombard, new lord
of Gourdon.

③ Chemin du Paradis is
the name given to the footpath
leading up to Gourdon.
The entire village is
marvellously fragrant, with
many craftsmen offering
perfumes, spun glass, olive
wood and Provençal artefacts.

④ Of its mediaeval castle,
Le Bar-sur-Loup has
preserved only the base of its
keep, standing in the middle
of the main square.
The church is dedicated to
Saint Jacques-le-Majeur and
its treasures include a great
altarpiece attributed
to Louis Brea.

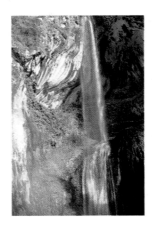

a sky cleared of all moisture, the land is cajoled with a thousand fragrances exhaled from among the rocks, under the trees and fields of tuberose, rose, carnation, jonquil, hyacinth and orange blossom. In its heyday, this "empire of the senses" spread over hundreds of hectares all the way to the outskirts of Cannes, Antibes and Nice. Each village has its own flower: violets in Tourrettes-sur-Loup, orange blossoms in Vallauris, etc. For infinite concentrations: 1 kg of essence of rose requires 12,000 kg of rose petals, i.e., 12 million roses. Originally, these droplets were used to scent leather, particularly the gloves fashioned in the voluble atmosphere of *Place aux Aires*. In bottles bearing the names of the best known brands (Dior, Guerlain, etc.),

1 *Gréolières: amid the ruins of Gréolières-Haute, Saint-Étienne church is typical of the Romanesque style of Provence, its single nave covered with a pointed barrel vault, a semicircular apse and bell cote on the side.*

2 *Cipières: the corn festival. The village, overlooking the valley at an altitude of 750 m above sea level, is located not too far from its fields of grain crops and pasture for livestock.*

they dazzle women in Paris, New York or Tokyo. In spite of the technical feats of the synthetic chemistry, nothing can replace jasmine flowers, picked at dawn with infinite care. The sudden accumulation of wealth narrowly contained in the ramparts can be deciphered in the maze of streets: refined townhouses, as gracious as in Aix-en-Provence, stand alongside rickety lopsided tenements with a door on each level, so steep is the slope. Still surrounded by gardens, Grasse with its wind-blown rooftops no longer garners the wheat and rye grown in the countryside and processed at its feet. Playing leapfrog between the drystone bories in the hills, may be the descendants of those who, on a chilly day in March 1815, saw Napoleon Bonaparte emerge from the scree, leaning on his staff.

Of that headstrong Emperor, who left his name to the *Route Napoléon,* there remain scattered memories: a stand of cypress trees in Roquevignon, a colonnade in Saint-Vallier-de-Thiey, Saint Martin's chapel in Escragnolles and the remains of Château de Brondet in Séranon. On the plateau of Caussols, the sky has washed and bleached the ground as nowhere else. Astronomers watch the slow gravitation of heavenly bodies. At their feet, the waters filter through the Earth's crust in bizarre funnels, excavating caves for spelunkers to explore or resurging in those curious wells near Saint-Cézaire. In this rocky landscape, amidst very ancient rock piles, bees busy themselves to fill the souvenir shops, brimming with honey, sweet scents, sachets of dried flowers, soaps, candles, etc. The geometrically landscaped garden of Gourdon, with its medicinal virtues, waits to heal the sufferings of lovers of infinity. Contrition may have led a hermit to seek refuge below, in the mossy meanders of the Loup River, where the poet Francis Ponge found unusual specimens of butterflies and fireflies.

2

ANTIBES AND ITS VICINITY:
the bashful

With its ramparts beaten by the surf announcing an armada, the starfish shaped "Fort Carré" (Square Fort) defending the bay and its two angular towers rising against the sky like the "two horns of a Barbarian's helmet", Antibes evokes a smaller version of Saint-Malo (in Brittany). Paul Arène found the town to be very tranquil in the early 20th century. It distinguishes itself from its neighbours for its position on the sea and its great age. Demographically, it hovers between second and third place, after Nice and Cannes. No one can question its archaeological primacy: before becoming the last link in the defensive line against Savoy, it was the first Greek colony between Marseille and the Alps. Today it is most appropriate that the

1 The harbour of millionaires: the oldest Greek colony between Marseille and the Alps, it was a commercial port until 1970. It is now one of the top yachting harbours in the Mediterranean, able to accommodate boats over 300 ft long. It attracts emirs and millionaires from all horizons.

2 The Fort Carré was built on a rocky promontory, on the site of a Temple to the Roman God Mercury. First a defensive tower in the 16th century, it was completed in 1585 by four bastions. The Fort was restored in 1967. With the Citadel of Villefranche, it illustrates the model of the first bastioned fortifications designed to resist artillery.

3 Aleppo pines have been prospering in Provence for 25 million years and cover over 200,000 hectares. With umbrella pines, they are among the most widespread trees on the Provençal coast.

1 *The old town of Antibes encompasses the two parts of the Citadel: the upper town, built on the site of the ancient Ligurian, Greek and Roman cities, and the lower town, built around the cathedral.*

city's original name, *Antipolis*, has become associated with another Greek word, *Sophia,* to designate Europe's oldest Science and Technology Park, built on some of that magical land haunted by the cicadas' song. What more fitting symbolic expression of the link between technological inventiveness and its cultural matrix? Already a precursor, Picasso had shed his light on the mythological dimension of these sites. In the course of a stay here following World War II, he refigured it in a sort of primordial inscription on a series of works bequeathed to the *Château-Musée* that now bears his name. The dialogue between Earth and Sea, begun under the gaze of Achaean gods, is pursued in the

triangle of Biot and Vallauris. Descendants of the first Ligurians or migrants from northern climes, artists and craftsmen burned with sacred fire the clay and silica wedded in delicate enamels. The potters' wheels keep turning, kilns are still fired and bubble glass is twisted into jewellery or shaped for the table or decoration. But the rounded sides of the great earthenware jars no longer hold oil or wine; their parentheses echo the typical Mediterranean lifestyle. Antibes was the last of the coastal cities, both literally and figuratively, to open to the fashion of tourism; the other resorts had preceded it in reputation. In haste, as often happens with latecomers, the town sacrificed half its ramparts at the

2 *The Cap d'Antibes peninsula between Antibes and Juan-les-Pins peaks at 75 metres above sea level and offers its splendid panorama and beautiful estates (Éden Roc, Château de la Croë, Eilen Roc, Villa Fiamma, etc.)*

turn of the 19th century; the other half watching the luxury yachts on *"Quai des milliardaires"*. But the exterior does not matter. The spirit remains, perpetuated by the *Commune Libre du Safranier* with its highly symbolic headquarters in a tavern behind the ramparts in the heart of the mediaeval city. Tourism did not lead a frontal attack on the city, it came from the Cap d'Antibes. There, blessed by La Garoupe sanctuary, "the most beautiful flowers in Europe were grown" and thousands of others acclimated. Villa Thuret preserves them under the watchful eye of INRA agronomers in white lab coats. Bringing botany under his control, Francis Meilland made his roses into the

1 *In the famous pine grove named after Frank Jay Gould in July, the Jazz festival, started in 1960 by Jacques Hebey and Jacques Souplet, attracts the most famous jazz musicians: Louis Armstrong, Ray Charles, Ella Fitzgerald, Colorante, Hampton, etc.*

2 *Biot: This rocky promontory was occupied as early as 154 BC by the Romans. Later, after invasions, plague and war, Biot was declared a "dead city" until the 14th century, when the village came back to life and the church was rebuilt. Pottery making remained the main source of wealth until 1918. The glassworks, opened in 1956, are now open to contemporary art.*

③ Glass blower in Biot.

④ Place de Valbonne: in the heart of the village, this fine arcaded square has preserved its 16th-century appearance and offers a hospitable setting with its cafés and restaurants.

③

*T*he Picasso Museum: the 16th-century stone castle houses a collection of ancient Roman sculpture. It was known under the name "Grimaldi", until a strange episode: the coming of Pablo Picasso, between August and December 1946. In this "encampment", to use Gilles Lapouge's term, the painter underwent a metamorphosis. The "tormentor" and the tormented, aggressive, tragic, turbulent "creator" of the Harlequins and "Guernica", discovered he had "a sudden new vocation for happiness". There were several reasons for this: the end of World War II, his new love Françoise Gillot, the birth of another child and, of course, "the jubilation of the place". For an obsessional artist like Picasso, who lived in each of the world's great painters, working in a sanctuary of art, a museum, was an exhilarating experience. Especially in a "land blessed by the gods, who, after two thousand years, still haunted the figures of that civilisation of happiness secreted by Pericles' Greece". The paintings and drawings that form a remarkable whole, one of the most complete for this artist, instil life into a world of whimsical goats, laughing fauns, centaurs and nymphs. He donated this treasure to the curator: 25 paintings on fibrocement and 44 drawings, subsequently completed by gouaches and more than 200 ceramic pieces from Vallauris. He had only one condition: that the collection remain on permanent display. Grimaldi could only bow down.

Vallauris: in 1946, Picasso fashioned his Little Faun *here and brought many other artists in his wake: Cocteau, Miró, Léger, Lurçat, Pignon, etc. A possession of the Abbey of Lérins since 1038, the village is first mentioned in 1138. Around 1500, after being ravaged by war and famine, it was repopulated by families from Italy who brought their skills with them: they made earthenware jars and cooking utensils. In 1700, Vallauris launched into the manufacture of fine Louis-XV style dishes. In the 19th century, more than a third of the population lived from pottery making.*

favourite messengers of love. Eilen Roc was the first residence built to its glory, and the high walls surrounding the estate remain silent on the whims of beautiful women, with or without aesthetes. The footsteps of magnates of finance or ephemeral stars of cinema can be heard treading on the gravel of Hôtel du Cap and Éden Roc. When the surf wanes on the rocks, when the sky is lit with stars above the "Goddess of the Sea" submerged a short distance away at Miró's request, jazz takes over from the cicadas in the Pine Grove. Since Frank Jay Gould launched Juan-les-Pins before World War II and Sidney Bechet blew his horn there after, the resort has ceased being a mere annexe of Antibes, to become a small enclave that has never lost its libertine ways.

1

2

The old town of Vence, the ancient Roman city of Vintium *founded in Augustus' reign. In the Middle Ages, Vence lost much of its importance. "Christian" Vence, loyal to the Catholic faith during the Wars of Religion, benefited from the prestige of its bishops, including Saint Véran in the 5th century, Saint Lambert in the 12th, Alessandro Farnese, elected to the Holy See as Pope Paul II, in the 16th century.*

2 *The "Baous" of Saint-Jeannet and La Gaude.*

3 *The Matisse chapel: "This chapel is for me the achievement of an entire life of work and the result of an enormous effort, sincere and difficult," said Henri Matisse, who designed and decorated the chapel as an expression of his gratitude to the Dominican nuns who had cared for him in 1943. In the white space, light plays through the yellow, green and blue stained glass and fills the chapel with colour. The altar is made of stone from Rognes.*

VENCE AND ITS VICINITY: the joy of living

3

Like "crouching sphinxes", the *"Baous"* stand side by side, the "Black" and the "White", buttressed against the winds and wintry weather blowing down from the Mercantour mountains. Their 300 metres of sheer bleached carcass offered to the hands and feet of the most daring climbers, they stand watch, good-naturedly, alongside their twins of La Gaude and Saint-Jeannet, over Vence and its vicinity, nonchalantly overlooking the sea. Over hill and dale, cypress, oleander, pine, willow trees seem to prosper here more than elsewhere, "copses so fresh you would think they are all leaning on the banks of an invisible river." Italy or Greece? a perfect synthesis, a blend of the wilderness of the Peloponnese and the gentle landscapes of Tuscany. Transparent air and silky light for artists. The great 17th-century painter Nicolas Poussin set them as

1 *The village of Bouyon. The church, dedicated to Notre-Dame de l'Assomption and Saint-Trophyme, was rebuilt after the big earthquake of 1887.*

2 "Village Nègre": *the karstic formations on Plateau Saint-Barnabé near Col de Vence, where the eroded limestone evokes an African village.*

3 Baou *de Saint-Jeannet overhanging the village of the same name, a haven for mountain climbers.*

the backdrop for his *Arcadian Shepherds*. Bounded by the ancient Roman *Via Aurelia*, Vence was prized by rich Romans for its wholesome climate. Then, like Nice, it became the See of a bishopric that would be the smallest in France, and has left many anecdotes. One of its bishops, Antoine Godeau, a famous 17th-century literary figure elected to the newly created *Académie Française,* left his name to a town square. On Place Godeau, the fountain, like the others disseminated in the city, sings the joy of this proudly Provençal cathedral town, with its fine Gothic stalls and its castle. In his *Chapelle du Rosaire*, Henri Matisse fashioned a final tribute to God, in white and blue, yellow and green, spiritualised "light, forced to cling to an act of faith." Nearby, stands Saint-Paul-de-Vence on its promontory. Preserved behind its ramparts like a ship's

The Maeght Foundation: Modern Art has its oasis and monastery among the tall pine trees and live oaks on Les Gardettes hill, which art lovers from the world over climb like pilgrims in the spirit of devotion. On the lawn punctuated with rustling anthropomorphic shapes, it is presided by a cornet of concrete through which the light pours into the white rooms. Joan Miró, Jean Arp, Marc Chagall, Jean Dubuffet, Fernand Léger, Bram Van Velde, Antonio Tapiès, Georges Braque and many others have left their mark on the walls, terraces and ponds Marguerite and Aimé Maeght created "instinctively and lovingly," as André Malraux would say. "The world in which modern art could find both its place and that other world that used to be known as the supernatural." In spite of the thousands of works of art and 13,000 volumes in the library, there is no claim here of ever being exhaustive. In addition to the permanent collections, so revealing of its founders' tastes, the major retrospective exhibition offered every summer, either around a single artist (Nicolas de Staël, Pierre Bonnard, Max Ernst, Francis Bacon, Henri Matisse, Otto Dix, etc.) or a theme ("art in motion", "the sculpture of painters"), is always a rich and meaningful event.

1 *The Maeght Foundation: Founded in 1964 by Aimé and Marguerite Maeght to exhibit the works of contemporary artists, the Foundation today is an absolute must for all aficionados of modern and contemporary art. In the gardens and inner courtyard, stand side by side sculptures by Giacometti, Calder, Miró, stained glass by Braque, a mosaic mural by Chagall... Inside, it offers a succession of prestigious exhibitions.*

2 *Saint-Paul: the fortified mediaeval village located on a rocky promontory wished to maintain its independence from the powerful city of Nice. In the 16th century, it became a major stronghold, retaining its military role until the end of the 19th century. The valley at its feet descends southward in terraces planted with orange, olive and pine trees.*

1 The old streets of Saint-Paul: The village, still surrounded by its rampart wall built in 1540, is a maze of steep narrow streets brimming with flowers, dark vaulted passageways and stone walls.

2 A fountain in Saint-Paul.

3 4 "Under the Royal Gate, the dust from the games of pétanque played at the foot of the plane trees..." From the beginning of this game of bowls, tradition has it that the team that loses 13 to nothing, kisses the "fleshiest" part of Fanny.

bow, it proved more resistant to the attack of the troops of Holy Roman Emperor Charles V than to the artists who now set up camp at *La Colombe d'Or*. For over half a century, the most famous painters have left their mark on the walls of this famous hotel and restaurant. Under the Royal Gate, the dust from the games of *pétanque* played at the foot of the plane trees recounts memories of Yves Montand, Jacques Prévert, Simone Signoret or Lino Ventura, who enjoyed engaging in this sport, which, though relatively effortless, is philosophically rich. Nestled in its splendid garden, the Maeght Foundation is a more serious pilgrimage for aficionados of contemporary art. But with their easels, colour-mongers have busily colonised the entire surrounding area: vertiginous Tourrettes-sur-Loup with its corbelled houses amid fields of violets,

54

5 *The Violet Festival in Tourrettes-sur-Loup: Violets were long the main source of livelihood for Tourrettes-sur-Loup. The flowers are picked in spring and sold fresh or to be crystallised in the region's sweets factories or in Toulouse.*

6 7 *All that remains of the rampart wall built in the Middle Ages around Tourrettes-sur-Loup are the houses overhanging the cliffs. Inside the 15th-century church dedicated to Saint Gregory the Great, the fine altarpieces include a panel painting sometimes attributed to Louis Brea.*

La Colle-sur-Loup, La Gaude or Saint-Jeannet. The most solitary steps will have taken them to Bouyon, Bézaudun, Carros or Le Broc. But these tender landscapes have their boundaries. Beyond Château Saint-Martin, the uppermost of the luxury hotels of the coast, a few hairpin turns lead to a strictly mineral universe, carved by wind, fog and rain. A source of inspiration surges even from this hard ground, lined with oak leaves. Coursegoules is the milestone towards another, Upper Provence. But, looking back nostalgically 180 degrees towards the sea, there stands the crenellated silhouette of the castle of Cagnes-sur-Mer, dashing under its crown of banners. It emerges from the checkerboard tiers of tiled roofs, concealing in the maze of narrow winding streets some of the region's finest restaurants. One can almost still hear

1 *Panoramic view on the sea from Col de Vence*

2 *The old village of Carros.*

3 *La Gaude, between the olive trees and the Baous.*

4 *The castle of La Gaude overlooking agricultural terraces*

5 *Village in the hinterland, Le Broc, against the backdrop of the snow-capped Alps*

Suzy Solidor's throaty voice singing of men and the sea to the end of the night. Her forty portraits adorning the walls of the castle recount more than a half-century of the history of painting, begun by Renoir in the olive grove of his home in Les Collettes. On the beaches of Le Cros de Cagnes, the last traditional boats, or *pointus,* unfurl their silvery nets for early-rising tourists. In nearby Villeneuve-Loubet, behind the undulating forms of Marina Baie des Anges, the disciples of Auguste Escoffier come in search of culinary secrets in the home of the inventor of that unforgettable dessert, Peach Melba. The Epicurean joy of Vence and its vicinity.

1 *The castle of Haut-de-Cagnes, now a museum of painting, sculpture and floral art, was built by the Grimaldis in the 14th century, and later embellished in the 17th century. It was purchased by the municipality in 1936 to house the museum. The village ramparts have preserved several 13th-century fortified gates.*

2 *Fishing for* poutina *(tiny fish fry) on the beach of Cagnes-sur-Mer.*

3 *An architectural serpent almost rising out of the sea, Marina Baie des Anges was built between 1968 and 1997.*

NICE AND ITS VICINITY:
the enigmatic

Who does not know Nice, if only by hearsay? The pure oval of its seafront, studded with turquoise or silver, according to the time of day, is celebrated round the world, and has been the fortune of photographers. Respectable or risqué, according to those who discover it. Like this showcase with its dual message, Nice conceals the obvious and becomes deceptive. Seeking the most appropriate epithets, ten come to mind: Sardinian, bawdy, Russian, bourgeois, Roman, aristocratic, Provençal, old-fashioned, British, mystic, Greek, untidy! And what more could I say? Its name, in spite of Audiberti's assertions to the contrary, has nothing to do with the Greek word for victory, but derives more likely from several sources. Yet today

1 *The very pure curve of Baie des Anges. Along its 8-km coastline, Promenade des Anglais rims Nice and the hills behind the city from the Airport to the West to the point of Rauba Capéu to the East, in tune with the majestic arc of Baie des Anges.*

2 *The dome of Hôtel Negresco, whose shape is said to have been inspired by the breasts of a famous turn-of-the-century actress, coifs this legendary Belle-Époque monument, the last example of the luxury hotel-museums in Nice, reflecting a certain gracious art de vivre made of typically French tradition and service.*

3 *The entrance to the Port of Nice, Rauba Capéu and part of Baie des Anges. In the foreground, the jetty on which Chekhov enjoyed strolling and the War Memorial designed by the architect Roger Seassol of Nice and inaugurated in 1928 by Field-Marshal Foch. In 1770, a trail was cut into the Castle Hill to reach the Limpia port from the South. It was broadened in the 19th century and in 1913 was named "Rauba Capéu", because the strong wind from the sea often swept away people's hats.*

1 *The Castle Hill seen from Mont-Boron. The hill, 93 metres high, was the site of the ancient* oppidum *occupied by Phocaean Greeks. Today, amid the park's luxuriant vegetation, ponds and artificial grottoes, few remains can be seen of the fortress destroyed by Louis XIV.*

the Paillon River, which inspired jibes from foreign visitors for its dry pebbles and instilled fear at times in those who lived along its banks, is encased under the flowerbeds honouring Field-Marshal Masséna and the marble of a mausoleum to the Arts. As it leads off into the sunset, Promenade des Anglais, on which a seagull casts the shadow of a four-engine jet, seems very much pressed for time for a Southerner. Hôtel Negresco times the cyclists, roller skaters and marathon runners as they go by. The palm trees prefer to ogle the bare-breasted sirens on the beach, who never frighten the "angels" in the Bay. There is no breach of morals here, since they are mere fish, some are caught with other snares, to end up on the terraces

of restaurants at Cours Saleya, the Port or the pedestrian street. On the hills, still spared by urban sprawl, flowers still bloom in greenhouses and vine grows on trellises. Saint-Antoine-de-Ginestière, Fabron, Saint-Pierre-de-Féric or Gairaut roll gently down towards the sea in a maze of tiled roofs and terraces punctuated with towers or bell cotes, some with bulbous domes. Rebellious to the ochre, glass and glazed tile, like an Italian-style plume, the verdant rock-borne citadel of the Castle stands out against the bay, virtual today, but scaled by history, only to be descended by legend. Two women come down to us from those legendary times, tutelary figures in the colourful, fragrant old town: Reparata, the saint who survives in the most splendid jewel of Baroque

② *The pebble beaches of Nice along Baie des Anges.*
"The people of Nice are influenced by the sea and the impiety of their beach, with its constant noise and thunder, due to the horrible movement of the pebbles," wrote the son of the famous astrologer Nostradamus in *his* History and Chronicle of Provence *in 1614.*
Nietzsche said: "I need the light, the air of Nice; I need Baie des Anges!"

1 *A play of shadow and light in a street in Old Nice. In the heart of the old town, the aristocracy of Nice built their palaces from the 17th to the 19th century, their architecture displaying strong influences from Genoa. Nice is clearly a Mediterranean city, its winding streets lined with tall narrow buildings. From the red-tiled rooftops emerge the bell towers of two of the seven Baroque churches in Old Nice.*

2 *The Port of Nice. It was in 1749 that excavation began on the Port, between Mont-Boron and the Castle Hill, but it was not until 130 years later than the Port reached the size it has today. First exporting olive oil and importing grain, then conveying lime, cement, coal and wood, the port began moving towards the accommodation of yachts and large cruise ships. Overlooking the harbour, Place Ile-de-Beauté has preserved its fine 19th-century façades, symmetrically arranged on either side of the Notre-Dame-du-Port church.*

Cours Saleya and Chapelle de la Miséricorde. Cours Saleya has a double life: a sunny side and a shaded side. Fruit and vegetable market, flower market, antiques on Mondays, and the early morning inevitable or historic cafés... Even in the wee morning hours, life never pauses here, on one of the world's most famous pedestrian areas. Chapelle de la Miséricorde, which belongs to the Confraternity of Black Penitents, was built in the 18th century. It is one of the loveliest masterpieces of Baroque art, with its elliptical nave and its beautiful Baroque-style decoration completed in the 19th century.

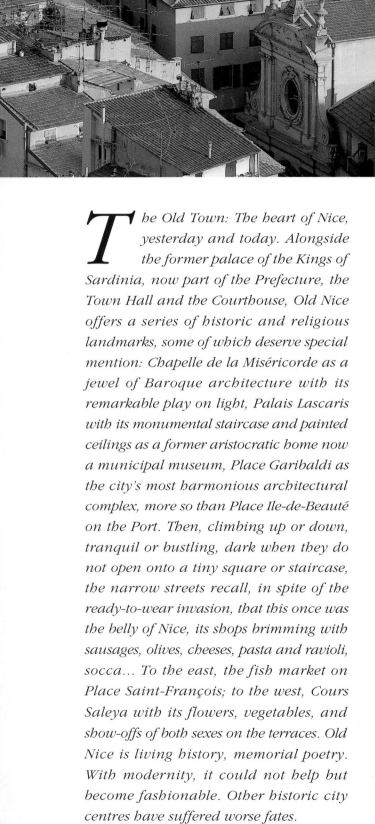

The Old Town: The heart of Nice, yesterday and today. Alongside the former palace of the Kings of Sardinia, now part of the Prefecture, the Town Hall and the Courthouse, Old Nice offers a series of historic and religious landmarks, some of which deserve special mention: Chapelle de la Miséricorde as a jewel of Baroque architecture with its remarkable play on light, Palais Lascaris with its monumental staircase and painted ceilings as a former aristocratic home now a municipal museum, Place Garibaldi as the city's most harmonious architectural complex, more so than Place Ile-de-Beauté on the Port. Then, climbing up or down, tranquil or bustling, dark when they do not open onto a tiny square or staircase, the narrow streets recall, in spite of the ready-to-wear invasion, that this once was the belly of Nice, its shops brimming with sausages, olives, cheeses, pasta and ravioli, socca... To the east, the fish market on Place Saint-François; to the west, Cours Saleya with its flowers, vegetables, and show-offs of both sexes on the terraces. Old Nice is living history, memorial poetry. With modernity, it could not help but become fashionable. Other historic city centres have suffered worse fates.

1 View of the rooftops of Old Nice from the Castle Hill. To the left, Rue de la Préfecture; in the back, the façade of the Saint Reparata's Cathedral restored from 1972 to 1982 by the fresco painter Guy Ceppa.

2 At the eastern end, Promenade becomes Quai des États-Unis, then Quai Rauba Capéu. It is from this point that one can enjoy the clearest and most classic view of the city and its seafront or of the vista to the top, including the Bellanda Tower, now a Naval Museum, where Hector Berlioz lived in 1844, and the hotels where Raoul Dufy painted Baie des Anges and the Castle Hill.

1 *Promenade des Anglais, Baie des Anges with the beaches, palm trees from the Canary Islands and Hôtel Negresco.*

2 *The blue chairs on the Prom', recently redesigned, are the legendary way to sit on Promenade des Anglais to contemplate the Mediterranean Sea.*

3 *Place Masséna with its pink façades, arcades, flowerbeds changing with the seasons, in a succession of blossoms, steps and fir trees. This is the true centre of life in Nice, and of its Carnival.*

4 *Esplanade du Paillon or Espace Masséna, covering 15,000 m², was inaugurated in 1983 after demolition of the former municipal casino. Today, it is a circular forum with a huge fountain and splendid waterworks.*

5 *Place Garibaldi. In the centre of the first major square in Nice, built in 1780 on the model of the great squares of Turin, France and Italy erected a monument in memory of Giuseppe Garibaldi in 1891. Born in Nice in 1807, he was an artisan of Italian unity and opposed the choice of the Comté de Nice to become French, which explains that his statue turns its back on Nice.*

1

1 *The MAMAC (Museum of Modern and Contemporary Art), designed by the architect Yves Bayard. Its four towers covered with marble of Carrara and connected by glass passageways make the museum look both massive and ethereal. From the terrace, there is a breathtaking view of the city.*

2 *The Élysée Palace includes in its façade two monumental statues of Venus by Sosno, caught in the hotel's granite walls: one looks towards the sea, the other is turned towards the hills.*

3 *'The Voyager', a sculpture by Max Cartier, 40 metric tons of stone and iron at the Riviera International Airport.*

4 *Jean-Claude Fahri's polymethacrylate sculpture, "Dissémination", graces the façade of Hôtel Nice Arénas across from the Airport. There are many other contemporary sculptures all over the city: Bernar Venet's "Arc" in Jardin Albert Ier, others by Arman, Gilli, Dolla, César, Calder, Borofsky, Klein... in front of the MAMAC and Acropolis Convention Centre, Sosno and Tobiasse at L'Arénas.*

5 *The Matisse Museum is a fine Genoan-style "Casa del Padrone", its red ochre walls festooned with 17th-century trompe-l'œil paintings. It was built on the ancient Roman site of Cemenelum, in a 36,000 m² wooded park planted with olive, pine, cypress and carob trees.*

architecture, and Catherine Ségurane, the heroine who defied the Turkish assailants. Nice pursues the struggle for its destiny and its identity. Hailed in all tongues, it mixes up its loyalties, "bestowing names from ancient Greece to American buildings": Acropolis, Arenice, Haliotis, etc. Its "Musicians' district" was rather the haunt of literary figures. The offices at L'Arénas gape onto a jungle. A port town, with being truly maritime, it became a seaside resort without losing its terrestrial penchant, although Nice sometimes dreams of gambling on the waves once more. But, as if to assert their identity, to flee the debilitating noise, fleeting time, its people run off in search of the joys of country roads, to Levens, Contes, Bendejun, L'Escarène, Peille, Lucéram. On a pilgrimage to Laghet where votive

1 *The Theatre of Nice was inaugurated in 1989. The octagonal shape outside, covered with marble of Carrara, contrasts with the warm tones of velvet, wood, leather and Venetian stucco inside, that contribute to the magic of the place.*

2 *The* Opéra *was built in 1885 by the architect François Aune on the site of the old* Théâtre Royal, *destroyed by fire. The façade, the building's majestic corner decoration, its staircase and the ceiling painted by Emmanuel Costa make it one of the finest such theatres in France.*

3 *In one place, on the same day,* La Grande Parade du Jazz *presents uninterrupted music on three podiums, such as a traditional jazz band in the Roman amphitheatre, a rock group in the olive grove and a Brazilian band in front of the Matisse Museum.*

4 *The Carnival of Nice: for over a century, in February, Carnival Parades, made up of 20 floats, 800 "big heads" and marching bands, have been prepared by dynasties of* Carnavaliers. *Famous artists, like Ben, César and many others also participate in Carnival.*

5 *In the* Batailles de Fleurs *held on Promenade des Anglais, elegant young women throw impressive amounts of flowers into the waiting crowd.*

1 Aspremont, with its concentric rows of houses, offers a splendid panorama from the terrace where the castle used to stand, 530 m above sea level.

2 Levens was founded in the 11th century. In 1621, the people rebelled against their lord. The village rises above a broad restful meadow.

3 Towering over Tourrette-Levens, the "Conque d'or" forms a verdant cirque where cereal was grown. The former castle houses a museum of butterflies.

4 Berre-les-Alpes has been occupied since Antiquity, as attested by archaeological remains. The village is surrounded by chestnut, pine and mimosa trees.

5 The village of Contes overlooks the Paillon River, which carried off part of the village in 1530, and again in the 18th century and in 1836. In the church, the altarpiece dedicated to Mary Magdalene is attributed to François Brea (16th century).

6 The listed historic village of Peillon, huddled on a peak 375 m above sea level, overlooks the Galembert stream.

7 Lucéram, the façades of its houses in a maze of narrow streets, has preserved remains of its 12th and 14th-century ramparts, Gothic houses and vaulted passageways. Until the 19th century, the village's main livelihood was from its olive trees and lavender.

paintings transmit the wisdom of yore, to the villages of Peille with its town hall in a former chapel or Coaraze whose many fascinating sundials capture the sunlight. A turbulent land with immobile villages: the Comté released, to its very heart, in spite of its eventful

Villefranche occupies one of the world's most beautiful bays. Charles of Anjou created the free port in 1295, as indicated by the name, "Villefranche". In the 16th century, Duke Emmanuel-Philibert of Savoy made Villefranche the arsenal for his galleys and, in 1557, the Mont-Alban fort overlooking Villefranche, and the Citadel and Bassin de la Darse below were built. The Bay is very deep (70 to 700 metres), which make it a strategic stopover for American warships. French, British and American military units can regularly be seen here along with more peaceful cruise ships.

2 3 *Beaulieu-sur-Mer was built on the site occupied by the port of Anao, Greek, then Roman. Huddled at the foot of a series of hills, Beaulieu enjoys a microclimate, the warmest in France, recognised and appreciated since Antiquity. It was a favourite haunt of the Grand-Duke of Russia, French Empress Eugénie, the Prince of Wales, rich industrialists and Hollywood stars.*

4 *Villa Kerylos is a dream built from 1902 to 1908 by Théodore Reinach, an eminent scholar and archaeologist, in tribute to ancient Greek civilisation.*

past and popularity. There survive the familiar ancestral practices, where the fêtes still have meaning, rooted in simplicity stripped of all the artifices of the coast. A touch of austerity, blended with golden oil, can be devoured with the eyes like happiness under

the chestnut trees. But when the rocky landscapes, with fire as their accomplice, take over once more, the Comté dashes towards the sea. The silhouettes of the cacti in the Exotic Garden of Èze are like strange hidalgos standing guard. Unless they are spying on the overly discreet comings and goings in the alleyways of Cap-Ferrat. Below in its verdant setting, Beaulieu remains the "pearl of the French Riviera",

1 *Saint-Jean-Cap-Ferrat was a fishermen's hamlet until the end of the 19th century. In the early 20th century, two financiers, then Leopold II became the main landowners on Cap-Ferrat, followed by the Duke of Connaught, Princess Helen of Serbia, etc. This carefree period was interrupted by war. At Saint-Hospice point, there is a trail that can be followed around almost the entire "millionaires' peninsula".*

[2] *Èze village, perched atop a rocky peak, overlooks the sea from its height of 427 m. The protohistoric* oppidum *and its Cyclopean wall of the Mont Bastide nearby are the remains of a Celto-Ligurian site, followed by a Roman settlement on the* Via Aurelia. *The stronghold was dismantled by Louis XIV in 1706 before being returned to Savoy. In 1860, the Comté de Nice voted by referendum to become part of France. Sentier Frédéric Nietzsche, the trail on which the philosopher is said to have found the inspiration for "Thus spoke Zarathustra", descends towards Èze-sur-Mer.*

of which Somerset Maugham complained that it distracted him from his work. The imposing citadel of Villefranche, encircled by bougainvillaea, clematis and bindweed, eyes the entrance to the bay. The narrow skiff of one of Paul Morand's readers glides between the cruise ships at rest, towards Hôtel du Cap, a witness of a grand century-old hotel tradition.

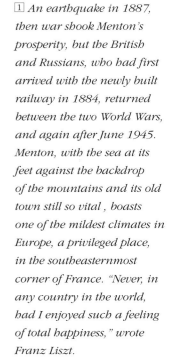

MENTON AND ITS VICINITY:
the mildest climate

At court, their imperial destinies suffered a sad fate. But in this land where Byron "wished to live", Elisabeth of Austria, better known as Sissi, and Eugénie de Montijo, who reigned by Napoleon III's side, experienced ineffable moments, in those magic gardens whose petals met by the spray. Even the cemeteries, where all of Europe is present everywhere, display no melancholy. "Adorable," exclaimed Gustave Flaubert, as he passed through. "No crosses, no tombs. The grass is tall and green." Perhaps, as some have written, this a foretaste of paradise! At the Vallonnet Cave, history waxes lyrical. From this, one of the oldest prehistoric sites in Europe, the million-

1 *An earthquake in 1887, then war shook Menton's prosperity, but the British and Russians, who had first arrived with the newly built railway in 1884, returned between the two World Wars, and again after June 1945. Menton, with the sea at its feet against the backdrop of the mountains and its old town still so vital , boasts one of the mildest climates in Europe, a privileged place, in the southeasternmost corner of France. "Never, in any country in the world, had I enjoyed such a feeling of total happiness," wrote Franz Liszt.*

2 *The Bastion was built in 1636 as part of the defences of Menton. It became a salt store in the 19th century, a gaol in 1940 and, in 1957, the poet and artist Jean Cocteau decided to use it to exhibit his works and it became the Cocteau museum in 1967.*

3 *Sosno's "Four Seasons" fountain on Place Saint-Roch (1996, marble of Carrara on a blue granite base).*

year-old remains, preserved in the Regional Prehistory Museum, suggest that this enclave was ready for the picking, even then. From Garavan mountain to the east to the village of Roquebrune to the west, tiny verdant valleys spring from their funnel-shaped valleys. They are topped by three villages linked by one of the six major hiking trails (GR, or *Grande Randonnée*) criss-crossing the département. Coming from Italy and heading towards the area of Nice, the GR 51 follows the "balconies on the Mediterranean". From their crow's-nests, Castellar, Sainte-Agnès and Gorbio form a sort of ancient chorus protecting these sites. Such perched habitats were long privileged for dwellings, before the people became so bold as to move closer to the sea

1 *Jardins Émile Biovès. The gardens, named for a former mayor of Menton, with their exotic plants and flowerbeds separating Avenue de Verdun and Avenue de Boyer, host the Citrus Festival every year in February.*

2 *The Baroque churches of Saint-Michel and La Conception, the White Penitents' chapel, overlook part of the old town, which rises to the old cemetery, built on the site of the mediaeval castle. In front of the red-tiled rooftops of the old town, a massif of bougainvillaea, which thrives only with an ideal combination of water and sunshine.*

Villa Fontana Rosa: The great red ochre and orange villa, with its bluish rendering and doors and windows set in brightly coloured faience tiles, disappeared from the Garavan slopes, as did its creator. He chose to end his days in Menton, said to be the "most poetic place on the French Riviera." Yet, any lyrical soul who approaches it can feel more of an absence than a void. That may be due to the encounter at the entrance to the estate of a famous European literary trio: Balzac, Cervantes, Dickens. But that is not all; everything in this blend of tropical and Mediterranean flora - the columns, the ponds, even when empty, the pergolas covered with climbing roses, the colourful planters, benches and especially the friezes, ceramic friezes everywhere, with fruit, flowers, animals - praises life, imagination, spirit, creation, writing... "This garden resembles Valencia, my Valencia, and reminds me at all times of the colours and smells of the gardens of my land." Of Vicente Blasco Ibañez, there remain books, memorable even for film buffs (The Blood of the Arena, The Four Horsemen of the Apocalypse, etc.), and this extraordinary garden. And the city is working on restoring all its glamour, as Greta Garbo, Colette or Rudolf Valentino knew it.

Thanks to its mild climate
and the presence of
the British, subtropical
species have been
acclimated here since
the end of the 18th century,
in such gardens as Jardins
de la Madone, *created by*
Sir Lawrence Johnston with
its water garden and
splendid staircase of
Florentine composition
flanked by little fountains
all the way to the house,
Le Clos du Peyronnet *or* Val
Rahmeh, *created by a British*
couple and transformed into
a botanical garden by
Miss Campbell in the 1950s.

below and the shores it had fashioned. From the sea came invasions. Ominous blockhouses, some open to visitors, prove that time has wrought no change. Castillon, shaken from its perch by an earthquake, relives as a home for leather-workers, engravers, painters, in an act of faith in survival; it has been called "the finest village in France". Never abdicating its dismasted castle, Sainte-Agnès remains "the highest coastal village in Europe" and climbing to its peak, 700 metres above sea level, is more than just a test of physical narcissism, it is a moment of sheer admiration for those forebears who made it a daily necessity. Planted at the birth of a child, the cypress trees marking benches and flowerbeds would serve to build the future

1 There remain many examples of some of the architectural masterpieces of that carefree time known as the Belle Époque.
The city offers an inventory of prestigious builders: Charles Garnier, Abel Glena, Alfred Marsang, Adrien Rey, Tersling, etc.

2 Villa Séréna, designed by Charles Garnier in 1880, was bequeathed to the City of Menton by Koenig, its last owner. Queens, artists, French President Coty came here to marvel at its magnificent panorama from the latticework tower and its many terraces planted with exotic vegetation.

home. At the height of the harvest season, an aromatic golden fluid wells up from the surrounding dales and floods the city of Menton. The fruit of the lemon has become the city's emblem, with the Citrus Festival at the end of winter in a potpourri of oranges, kumquats, grapefruit, etc. Transformed for the sole pleasure of the eyes, the Biovès gardens mirror the fine exhibitions

3 Menton's covered market with its glazed tile decoration.

4 The friezes, dating from 1860 to 1930 and typical of this popular art form in Menton, are currently being restored under the supervision of the Monuments Historiques.

1 Fête du Citron. *Created in 1875, the Carnival of Menton became the Citrus Festival in 1934. In Jardins Biovès, giant designs made with lemons and oranges recount a different story each year with some fifteen floats.*

2 *The mediaeval village of Roquebrune-Cap-Martin, perched 300 metres above sea level, clings to the mountainside, in the shadow of its castle, built by the Counts of Ventimiglia, and subsequently modified by the Grimaldis of Monaco. Cap-Martin below was a favourite haunt for 19th-century aristocrats, with its sumptuous villas (Cyrnos, Aréthuse, Trianon, Del Maroe).*

in Palais de l'Europe nearby. In the streets, the brightly coloured mobile tapestries add fleshy tones to the ochre of the 19th-century façades. Botanists, professional and amateur, like the writer Blasco Ibañez, have left behind them the finest series of gardens on the entire Riviera. The profusion of vegetation rivals the architectural

1 Gorbio is perched atop a peak dominated by Mont-Agel (1,150 m). The village belonged to the Counts of Ventimiglia until the 12th century, then to the Counts of Savoy and finally to the Lascaris family, who sold their rights to the community in 1522.

2 Castillon. This strategically located village was destroyed in the War of Austrian Succession in the 18th century, then by an earthquake in 1887. After being relocated, it was razed to the ground in 1944. Five years later, it was rebuilt lower down and, since 1989, has become an artists' colony "Les Arcades du Serre", which holds symposia on the arts.

⒊ *Sainte-Agnès,* *the highest coastal village in Europe just 4 km from the sea as the crow flies, turns its back on Menton and faces the slopes of Pic de Baudon (1,264 m). From its cobbled streets with small squares and vaulted passageways, a trail leads up to the ruins of the old village and its castle, which once belonged to the Counts of Ventimiglia. The 20th-century Fort of Sainte-Agnès, open to visitors, was part of the defence system of the Maginot line.*

exuberance. The most fortunate visitors are those who come in September when these marvels, from Val Rahmeh to Domaine des Colombières, from Maria Serena to La Serre de la Madone, open their doors to unveil their splendid settings, where eternity vies with the ephemeral.

MONACO:
Home to a Prince

It all began on a dark winter night in 1297. A soldier disguised as a monk made his way into the fortress... It is hard to imagine this scene as you contemplate the Princely palace today. It is something out of a fairytale, guarded by "an army 130 strong, whose fine uniforms are never spoiled in the tough profession of war." The Changing of the Guard, at noon sharp, draws applause from the motley crowd massed in front of the palace in the hope of catching a glimpse of a Princess at the window. 700 years of history whose beginnings could have inspired a Verdi opera and which ends like a work by Johann Strauss. "In the middle of the village is a palace, in the middle of town a Casino. In the palace reigns a Prince, in the Casino

1 The palace of the Grimaldis lit up, its three crenellated towers evoking the 13th-century fortress. The castle was remodelled into a Renaissance palace in the 16th century, and again in subsequent centuries.

2 The Changing of the Guard draws crowds every day at noon.

3 General view of the Rock with the Princely Palace, the Immaculate Conception Cathedral and ochre houses, Fontvieille with the Louis II stadium and its modern buildings, part of the harbour built early in the 19th century and the rocky peak of Tête de Chien overlooking Monaco.

reigns a god: luck." That same luck led to the shooting of a Hitchcock film... Yet, it must be understand that, between Franceschino Grimaldi's daring assault and Prince Rainier III's wedding with a beautiful Hollywood actress, nothing has ever been random in Monaco's trajectory. Indeed, the Principality has come a long way. Barely more than a century ago, on this the rocky, marshy land, a few scrawny goats gnawed the frail olive trees of "the poorest State in Europe". Today, it has become "a huge, diamond-studded nugget" crowned by the oldest dynasty still reigning on the Continent. Under the tutelary patronage of Hercules and Saint Devota, Monaco owes a great deal to ladies, whose everyday actions were carefully followed at the

1 *These gardens, the site of an exhibition of contemporary sculpture held every two years, follow the gentle slope down to the Monte Carlo Casino, inaugurated in 1862. Since the Belle Époque, its gaming rooms have attracted many famous names.*

2 *The Casino terraces are graced with modern sculptures, like Botero's "Woman smoking" or Mitaraj's "Le Cuirassé".*

3 *View of the Casino from the sea. Today's Casino was built in 1878, in place of an earlier structure erected in 1863. It includes the opera house designed by Charles Garnier, architect of the Paris Opéra. The Atrium vestibule was decorated by Jules Dutrou with 28 stone columns. In 1881, Charles Garnier built "Salle des Amériques". The Casino was remodelled several times in the 20th century.*

Court of France, as they are today by the readers of gossip columns. Thus, Princess Caroline decided to open the very first, if modest, Casino on the French Riviera in 1861. On this rugged limestone plateau, a few years later, another woman, the commoner Marie Blanc and her husband, erected the building we know now, at the heart of what would become the bustling city of Monte Carlo. But, following in Sacha Guitry's footsteps down the splendid flower-decked *Allées des Boulingrins*, we can enjoy the permanent spectacle. Elegant Italians merrily walk under the famous wrought-iron marquee into the Atrium. Gleaming with all its chandeliers, it opens towards the ornate Opéra or the gaming tables of the Casino. Fascinating! From

1 *Hôtel de Paris, founded in 1864 by François Blanc, a millionaire from Homburg, was designed on the model of the Grand Hôtel on Boulevard des Capucines in Paris. Because its luxury and fine restaurant made it so successful, it has to be expanded repeatedly.*

2 *The 1,500-m² cellar, excavated in the bedrock, holds 250,000 bottles of great vintage wines on 1 km of racks and oak tuns full of aged cognac*

3 *The naiads and tritons in the lobby, their polychrome decoration gleaming under the glass roof, illustrate the Principality's maritime vocation.*

4 *The Belle Époque room in Hôtel Hermitage was decorated at the turn of the century by Gabriel Ferrier.*

5 *The glass roof over the winter garden was designed by Gustave Eiffel.*

6 *Hôtel Hermitage, inspired by the Grimaldis' palace, was built in 1900 on the site of a small inn surrounded by a grove of fruit trees.*

The Oceanographic Museum. Related in its monumental nature to that of Wall Street, this temple is not dedicated to money but to the scientific study of the sea, over which it towers from its height of 85 metres. Made of stone from the quarries of La Turbie, like the Trophy erected there in the time of the Roman Emperor Augustus, it materialised the dreams of Prince Albert I of Monaco for the "blue waters that conceal the mystery of our origins." A sailor and a scholar, he left fabulous collections of objects, nacre and animal specimens from his many campaigns at sea at the turn of the century. Open to research with its rich library, its laboratories and the Aquarium displaying coral and Mediterranean ecosystems, it is the most popular cultural site on the Riviera. The Micro-Aquarium, for the observation of microorganisms just millimetres long, enlarged some 3,000 times on a giant screen, adds yet another dimension to this institution. Prince Rainier III has followed in his ancestor's footsteps, giving the Principality a pilot role in preserving the environment and animal species, particularly vulnerable in the Mediterranean.

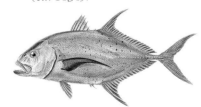

1 *Spitsbergen, 1899. The staff of the* Princesse Alice II *photographed by Prince Albert I of Monaco.*

2 *The skeleton of a finback whale grounded on the Ligurian coast in 1896.*

3 *Boarfish* (Capros aper) *and snipefish* (Macrorhamphosus scolopax) *that the Museum staff is alone in the world to have succeeded in preserving.*

4 *Tropical ecosystems are reconstructed in the Museum Aquarium.*

5 *Sea dragons are among the rarest specimens on display in the Aquarium.*

6 *In the Micro-Aquarium tiny fauna can be observed live. A shrimp (total length: 1 cm).*

Below, Trevally drawn by Oudart during a voyage around the world (ca. 1836).

[1] *Café de Paris, then a "café-divan" created by François Blanc in 1868 offering a coffee room, billiards, perfumery, cigars and tobacco from the start, was rebuilt several times before being transformed and restructured in 1988.*

[2] *Salle Garnier, designed by Charles Garnier of the Paris Opera House, was inaugurated on January 25, 1879, by Sarah Bernhardt. Raoul Gunsbourg was General Manager of the Opera House until 1951.*

[3] *The tenors Luciano Pavarotti, José Carreras and Placido Domingo on the stage of the Opéra de Monte Carlo.*

a limousine with smoked-glass windows gliding around the square, a merry widow enters the Hôtel de Paris lobby. Leather and mirrors. A meeting place. A shipping tycoon? Invitation to the *Louis XV*; a restaurant fit for a King, and below, in the cellars, the greatest vintages fill a full kilometre of wine racks. Thrilling! On the Café de Paris terrace, golden-tanned businessmen in coat-and-tie sip their drinks as they discuss their accounts and balance sheets, without missing a word of the chatter of the glamorous nymphets at the next table. Perhaps the Y2K Gigi, who knows? The valets busy themselves indifferently near Hôtel Hermitage, built around its winter garden. Although somewhat on the side, the *Sporting* remains the nerve centre of a gambling and entertainment empire, still controlled,

after over a century, by the SBM *(Société des Bains de Mer),* all the way north to the golf course perched on the Mont-Agel, east to the Larvotto point built on the sea for the galas at the *Monte-Carlo Sporting Club,* a must for the jet set *(Bal de la Rose* or the *Red Cross Gala),* and west, towards Cap d'Ail, the World Festival of the Circus in Fontvieille. This is the most recent of the Principality's districts. There is no magic in its origins; it is supported on 500 posts set on the sea floor

1 *General view of the Principality of Monaco.*

2 *The port was built in 1903 with 400,000 m³ of stones and 1,855 wooden posts, 8 to 16 metres long, because of its 40-metre depth, which can accommodate large yachts.*

3 *The Larvotto beach.*

4 *The new Port in the Fontvieille district, built on the sea to extend the Principality towards the south. The big tent at the foot of the Rock hosts the International Festival of the Circus and many trade fairs.*

5 *The Exotic Garden was created in 1913 and inaugurated twenty years later. It occupies a sun-drenched cliff protected from the wind, ideal for growing cacti, such as* Myrtillocactus geometrizans, *which reaches a height of 13 metres and weighs 1 metric ton.*

6 *In the foreground, some of the 23 tennis courts of the Monte Carlo Country Club, where the Monte Carlo Open Tournament is held every year in April; in the middle, the Monte Carlo Beach Hotel complex with its beach, built by the Société des Bains de Mer in the 1930s; in the background, Cap-Martin.*

at a depth of 40 metres. It is occupied by clones of the residential towers and office buildings around which the Formula 1 racing cars slalom for the Grand Prix. Thanks to the influence of its tutelary demigod, the Principality fears neither the wrath of the sky, with its high-rise buildings towering over neighbouring Beausoleil, nor the sea, nor the Earth, digging deep into its entrails to find new space for expansion. Without ever losing its identity, ever unique and desirable.

The original cradles of humankind. Two hundred years after the first winter visitors, tourists continue flocking to the hinterland for the region's mild climate, more recently for water sports, less so for the mountains. Although "green" tourism is gaining in favour and the mountains are ever present here, they are somewhat forgotten. Too discreet perhaps, they recall those stage sets designed with so much talent, they remain a mere backdrop that does not draw attention away from the foreground. How many visitors have discovered them too late, their to regret? From the coast between Antibes and Nice, in clear weather, preferably in winter, the silhouette of the mountains with their sugary caps stands out against the sky, sharp, powerful, majestic. They cannot be easily approached. Although they were formidable builders, the Romans preferred to build their great roadways to the *"Narbonensis"* across the lowlands. These walls of rock served as armour, dissuading aggressors, protecting the Ligurians from predatory invaders. They conceal the valleys, forming impressive notches, eroded by the waters caught in those splendid narrow gorges called *clues*. No entry! Not until the end of the 19th century did mechanical equipment bite into these natural features, excavating roads along the valley floors and altering millennia of tradition. The coastal towns grew in arrogance towards the mountains, which had supplied them with everything: cheese, meat, bread, wool, wood, leather, etc. The coast merely was "a perfumed wench with the superfluous, not the essential." But so much effort was required of farmers to eke out a living in their high-perched villages, walking through beech, fir and chestnut forest, making the best of the slightest flat ground and, where there was none, fashioning narrow terraces supported by those drystone walls called *"faïsses"*. All too easily confused with other older, more massive heaps of stone - the protohistoric *castellaras* - they inspired the writer Stendhal's admiration for "the patience of those poor peasants who piled up those desolate stones." There is even more emotion in a native son like Louis Nucéra, for whom they are not anonymous. "How many times, gazing on an isolated barn clinging to a peak or abandoned *restanques* [agricultural terraces] which had been so difficult to make fertile, I thought of their courage, their exhausted bodies, their silhouettes sleepwalking in the glow of dawn or twilight?" The fruits of this labour, sometimes seen to by their descendants, were described with lyricism by Maurice Toesca of Menton. "The soil of these terraces probably harbours the virtues that metamorphose a tomato into a delicious fruit, a tiny olive into a reservoir of a few drops of delectable gold, a fig into a spoonful of jam, a sprig of lavender into perfume extract that, when distilled, fill the entire valley with their evening fragrance." It was, however, less for defensive reasons than because the valley floors were so inconvenient and inhospitable, with flash flooding and the requirements of the agropastoral life, that the people were led to perch so high their "mediaeval villages as proud as chamois and, like them, smitten with the abrupt peaks," of which Auvare and Granile are among the most authentic examples. Solidarity was more than a mere word. Like the community gathered to slaughter a pig or for the harvest, the houses huddled together behind their thick walls to stave off the cold or keep in the fresh air, often at the foot of the castle, now in ruins. While today many of these narrow streets descend the lonely slope towards the fields, the cowbells are home to spiders and the chapel at the end of the valley is visited only by the boldest hikers. A few courageous souls have remained behind. Others have come in search of freedom to fashion cheeses with their own hands. But far too many have gone off to the cities. The old folks wait, perhaps for a day when the same technology that emptied their mountains brings life back, though teleworking and those strange typewriters called computers.

HE HINTERLAND

Sea, mountains and heritage on the French Riviera

THE ROYA VALLEY:
the valley of sound and colour

Mauve shale of the bedrock, ochre rendering of the façades or rust of leaves: the dominant family of shades, all related to red. This is the endpoint of an itinerary begun in the West, with the reddish glow of the Estérel Mountains. The Roya flows in the eastern end of the Alpes-Maritimes, its lower course beyond the borders of the département, since it spews its waters off Ventimiglia. This escapade into Ligurian territory does not suffice to explain visitors' feelings: not quite Italy and no longer completely France, somewhere in between, in the midst of magical sites, architecture, shapes and, of course, colours and sounds. Relatively spared by the invasion of modernity, this magic has persisted since the end of the Middle Ages, when Nice became the Count of Savoy's only outlet

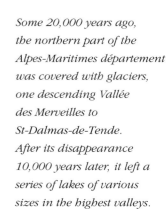

Some 20,000 years ago, the northern part of the Alpes-Maritimes département was covered with glaciers, one descending Vallée des Merveilles to St-Dalmas-de-Tende. After its disappearance 10,000 years later, it left a series of lakes of various sizes in the highest valleys.

1 Lac de Casterino is a reservoir 1,500 m above sea level. Surrounded by larch forest, this shallow lake attracts hikers and picnickers to its grassy shores.

2 The Roya river near the town of Breil. The torrent takes its source from the slopes below the Col de Tende, nearly 2,000 m above sea level and empties its waters into the sea in Ventimiglia, Italy. Its main tributary is the Bevera.

3 Canoeing down the Gorges of Saorge on the turquoise waters of the Roya. The narrow karstic faults form vertiginous clues, with sheer bluffs and rock shelters.

1 Breil-sur-Roya, built on
a bend in the river, boasts
remarkable civilian
and religious monuments.
Italianate influence is
everywhere, in the houses' red
and ochre façades decorated
with trompe-l'œil painting, the
wrought-iron balconies and
the Baroque church with its
glazed tile roof.

2 Piène-Haute, perched
613 m above sea level, became
French in 1947. Paved streets
rise towards the ruins of the
castle, perched on a strategic
site overlooking the Roya river.

3 Bergue Supérieur and
Bergue Inférieur, on either side
of the little valley of Bergue,
are hamlets of Saorge.

4 *Saorge. This village, built in the 11th century, 550 m above sea level, was fortified by the Dukes of Savoy. Defended by several forts, this mountain fastness enjoyed a strategic position as a barrier blocking access to the Roya valley. During the French Revolution, Saorge was captured by treachery in April 1794 and its ramparts destroyed, thereby opening the road into the Piémont.*

5 *La Brigue, the ancient Roman town of Brigantio, built 765 m above sea level, became part of France only in 1947 by an overwhelming 98% majority vote). Its pastoral economy supplied wool for marketing in Marseille.*

onto the sea and the departure point for the old "Salt Road". While the other valleys, deprived of so vital a justification, remained withdrawn inward, the upper Roya valley became a Royal Road to convey to Turin this precious condiment so crucial for food and so many other uses. Over the mountain passes of Braus and Brouis, then comfortably up to Italy, it is hard as you drive along the road to imagine the wild adventure it used to be: caravans of mules over your head, their cumbersome progression on trails overhanging bubbling rapids, slipping in the snow. It may be more poignant for hikers to sense the power of these landscapes with their sombre grandeur and the hardships of body and soul expressed in the heartfelt votive offerings in the local sanctuaries, foremost of

1 Pont du Coq, *a bridge near La Brigue, with mediaeval foundations.*

2 *The Baroque church of Fontan (17th century), with its lovely church tower and campanile.*

3 *Mediaeval festival in the Roya valley.*

110

4 *Steam locomotive on the Nice-Cuneo railway. After much prevarication starting in 1851, the works on the railway (through Sospel and the Bevera valley by excavating a tunnel under Mont Grazian) began on January 26, 1910, urged on by the Italians who had already pierced the 10-km long railway tunnel under the Col de Tende in July 1898.*

5 Lacs des Pasteurs *(2,230 m above sea level): from the grassy shores of these twin lakes, there is a view of the north face of Mont Bego, dominating the entire cirque of Fontanalba.*

which is Laghet, or the frescoes of Notre-Dame-des-Fontaines. Equally moving are some abandoned remains, like the old bridge across La Lavina, known only to the many white-water sportsmen who flock to the valley, or Notre-Dame-des-Grâces chapel near Breil. But the feast day of Saint Éloi, the mule drivers' patron, remains a tradition very much alive in Tende. Stopovers for a tourist route before it became the fashion and travellers not all of whom were miserable wretches, the towns used the green or mauve schist like coloured rendering in a display of decorative imagination, still a delight for the eyes. With their churches' oversized naves, Sospel, which still has its toll bridge across the Bevera river, and Breil, whose bridge was bombed during the Second World War, elegantly combine

To the strains of organ music: A Bach toccata or a Haendel concerto can be heard in the Sunday air of La Brigue or Saorge. This may seem surprising to uninformed visitors, unless they have already had the same experience in Fontan or Tende. This is the valley of organs. As if by a secret correspondence, the Roya Valley invested in these instruments what Brittany fashioned in its parish enclosures: stone, like wood, tin and copper, uplifts the soul and rejoices the senses. In reaction to the repression of the Protestant Reform, the lyrical exaltation of the Baroque, so splendidly expressed in the Comté de Nice in the 17th century, maintained itself very late in this valley. There, the time was taken to cover religious structures with stucco, gold leaf, friezes and cherubs, then install the sumptuous carved organ cases over the keyboard on which were played, during the services, transcriptions of bel canto and other operatic arias. Built by the three best Italian organ makers and brought in from Bergamo or Pavia, sometimes through the generosity of the Confraternities of Penitents, this series of six organs is unique. Thanks to the efforts of the organist René Saorgin and the excellent quality of the musical events organised here, they have deservedly inspired renewed interest.

1 Saorge: the keyboard of the organ in the Baroque church.

2 La Brigue: the organ built by the Lingiardi brothers (1849) in the 15th-century St-Martin church.

3 Breil-sur-Roya: the organ case (1863) in the Baroque church of Sancta-Maria-in-Albis, one of the finest in the Comté de Nice.

4 The organ case in St-Sauveur church built by the Lingiardi Brothers in 1847.

5 Tende: the old Salt Road went through the Countship of Tende, acquired by the Dukes of Savoy in 1579. It was the fastest route for mule trains conveying the precious substance from Nice to the Piémont over the Col de Tende. The town became French in February 1947 after the overwhelming success of a referendum, 2,603 in favour, 218 against.

6 Musée Départemental des Merveilles opened in Tende in July 1996. The museum displays replicas of the Bronze Age pictographs around Mont Bego.

7 Saint Éloi's feast in the streets of Tende. Every year in July, richly harnessed mules are led to the church to be blessed.

8 A street in Tende. The village, huddled on a very steep rise around the castle built by the lords, the Lascaris, later spread down to the banks of the Roya river.

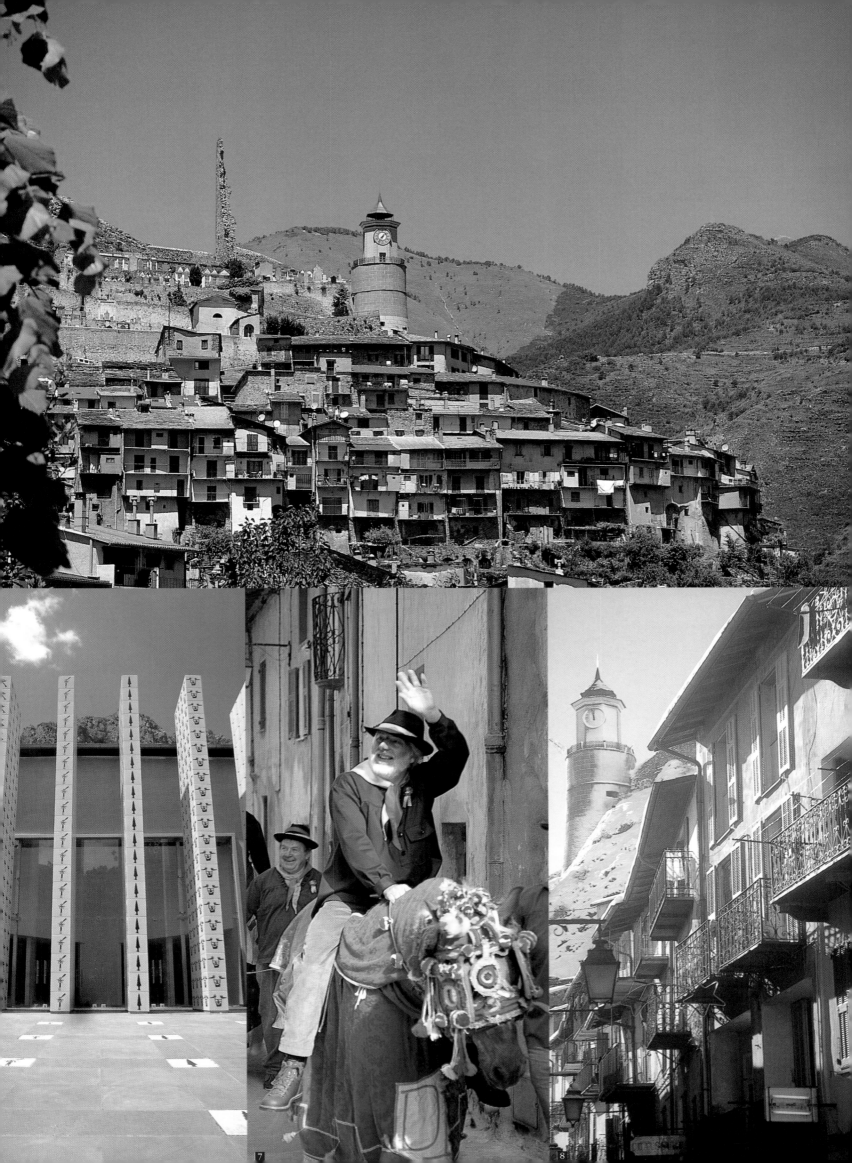

7

8

religious art and secular urban planning. Dubbed "little Gibraltar" for its strategic position, Saorge displays a striking balancing act with its triptych of religious and military edifices. Alternately a factor of unity and of dispute, the Roya bristles with massive tortoises that no longer fire on those approaching them. Along with the deepest cave in the Alpes-Maritimes (580 m), La Brigue offers a remarkable series of decorated lintels recalling the region's strong pastoral vocation. From the modest magnificence it once knew, the Roya valley displayed an ultimate show of coquettish pride: following the example of Tende, each town decided to acquire a fine Italian organ. Where else could such splendid harmony be found than along this musical river unique in France?

① *The old Salt Road to the Col de Tende was used from the Middle Ages to the 19th century by mule-drivers conveying salt from Nice to the Piémont and Lombardy. Muleteers formed an important guild whose patron was Saint Éloi.*

② *Sea of clouds in the Upper Roya valley.*

114

3 *Military works, armoured concrete blockhouses, were excavated along the 120 km of border. This one in the Bevera valley was part of the Maginot Line built (1922 to 1932) to defend the border from the Restefond Pass (the highest in the Alpes-Maritimes) to the St-Louis bridge in Menton.*

4 *Sospel was occupied by the Romans (Cespedellum) in ancient times. It was part of Provence in 1258, then of Savoy until 1861 when it became French. The old bridge, Pont de la Loge, spanning the Bevera river was first built in the 11th century. It was a toll station on the old Salt Road connecting the town's mediaeval core to the Saint-Nicolas district on the other side of the river.*

THE VÉSUBIE VALLEY:
the "Little Switzerland" of

"*La Suisse Niçoise*", Little Switzerland, another formula that has been round the world! An expression coined by Stephen Liégeard, the man who also invented the name *"Côte d'Azur"*. Not only was he captivated by the French Riviera, he also had the curiosity of looking beyond its coast, to leave us the description of what now seems obvious: "so striking are the similarities with William Tell's homeland that it is perfectly justified to bestow on this lofty region the nickname of Little Switzerland." The peaks encasing the valley are among the highest in the Alpes-Maritimes: Gélas (3,143 m), Chafrion (3,073 m), Malédie (3,059 m), Clapier (3,045 m). When Alpinism was still in its infancy, they attracted thrill-seekers and one of its pioneers, Count Victor de Cessole of Nice. Yet, Saint-

1 *The Vésubie, 48 km long, is formed upstream by the Boréon, Gordolasque and Madone de Fenestre, with its source at the foot of Mont Gélas (2,300 m above sea level). Thanks to these three torrents the Vésubie has enough water to supply the city of Nice throughout the summer (250 m³/second on average).*

2 *Mont Gélas from a helicopter: the highest point in the Alpes-Maritimes département, 3,143 m above sea level, 40 km from the sea. The IGN survey maps show the Vésubie's source at its foot, in* Lac Blanc.

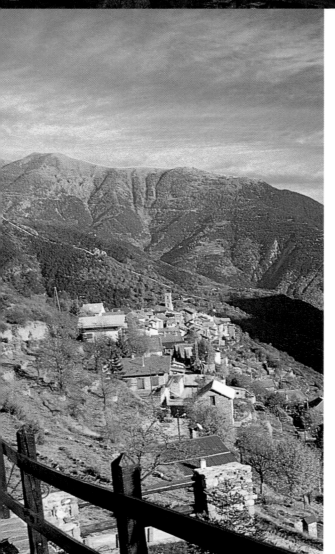

1 *Saint-Martin-Vésubie is a beautiful village in the* "Suisse niçoise", *near the finest peaks in the Alpes-Maritimes and the Mercantour National Park. In the late 19th century, it was already popular as a summer resort for the people of Nice. In the middle, the Baroque church of Notre-Dame-de-l'Assomption houses a panel painting attributed to Louis Brea.*

2 *The village of Venanson, built on a very narrow rocky promontory 1,164 m above sea level under the ridge of Spivol (1,350 m), overlooks the upper Vésubie valley.*

3 *Barns on the heights near Venanson.*

4 *Trout fishermen in the
Boréon, in the background
the grassy slopes
surrounding the lake are
covered with larch, the
best-known Alpine tree,
one of the few conifers to lose
its leaves in winter. It yields
excellent wood and can
live 500 years.*

5 *Waterfall in
the Boréon valley.*

6 *Saint-Martin-Vésubie
in the snow with Cime
de la Palu.*

Martin-Vésubie is a departure point for family outings and other, more adventurous hikes to the Mercantour range around it and opens slightly with the Boréon lake, a favourite of fishermen. Yet it has nothing of a high mountain resort, especially when seen from Venanson, which offers the most stereoscopic panorama over the village. In spite of its alpine features, this charming holiday resort is picturesquely and irremediably typical of Nice. Nestled in the hollow of a vast amphitheatre with rather gentle slopes and countless springs surging from among the chalets, it gathers them burbling in a gutter that runs down the middle of its main street. It is alone in the Southern Alps, with the fortified town of Briançon, to have retained this characteristically mediaeval trait. Like so

1 *Le Ponset (2,828 m) was used for location shots in the film* "La Croisière Jaune", *set in the Himalayas.*

2 *Roquebillière:* "In Rocabellera" *is mentioned in 1147. Built at the foot of the mountain, the village was destroyed in 1564 and again in 1926 by a mudslide, after which its population moved to the other side of the river.*

3 *The tiers of houses in the village of Lantosque overlooking the Vésubie.*

4 *La Bollène-Vésubie, 650 m above the Vésubie valley, has long been a popular summer resort.*

many other places in this territory, the Vésubie cannot be captured by a definition. It can be likened to the *Barbets,* cousins of the Chouans of Brittany, those rebels against the proponents of the French Revolution. This valley is where they concentrated their forces to resist the Jacobin invaders. Like Switzerland, or perhaps even more the Oisans or Valais mountain ranges, it boasts a great green wilderness. Grasping you as soon as you enter the gorges, it is particularly memorable between Le Cros d'Utelle and Lantosque with its curious *Grotte des Limaces* (Snails' Cave) in the little valleys of L'Infernet and Le Figaret. Dark waves of walnut and chestnut trees cling to the steepest slopes, revealing the shoals growling through their foliage. But "suddenly a group of houses, their brown roofs cemented with red

[1] *Saint-Jean-la-Rivière overlooking the Vésubie whose waters are harnessed here to supply the city of Nice.*

[2] *Le Cros d'Utelle (from the Provençal cros for hollow) is a hamlet in the commune of Utelle.*

122

3 *The village of Belvédère, with its traditional houses decked with balconies, overlooks the Vésubie valley from a broad promontory 830 m above sea level.*

4 *Saint-Dalmas-Valdeblore: Located 1,300 m above sea level, this beautiful mountain landscape was already populated in Gallo-Roman times. The village bears the name of the evangelist of the Alps and the parish church is dedicated to the Holy Cross. It was a priory with monks until the French Revolution in 1790.*
The village was once surrounded by a rampart wall, some of which remains in place.

mortar, form with the nearby cypress trees and chapel crowned with a cupola a delightful Italianate landscape evocative of some corner of the Roman countryside." Colourful Belvédère becomes fragrant with the autumn Shepherds' Festival. In winter, the hairpin bends to La Bollène, which continue on to the snow-covered roads of Turini, have long provided the moment of truth for drivers in the Monte-Carlo Automobile Rally Race. But the Vésubie valley is also home to the Madonnas who keep watch alongside its course. Looming over Utelle, Notre-Dame-des-Miracles has left the terraces and their olive trees for its windblown plateau, directly under the sky from which the stars seem to fall. At the upper end of the valley, Notre-Dame-de-Fenestre clings to Vallée des Merveilles in yet another mystery.

*T*he Via Ferrata *of La Colmiane.
With their jagged ridges and
rugged peaks, the Alpes-Maritimes
are reputed to be ideal terrain for
mountaineering. Those who wish to emulate
insects and scale vertical slopes come from
very far away to brave the hundreds of
routes on the Baou of Saint-Jeannet, La
Loubière near Monaco, La Roquette, La
Colle... Yet there is another intrepid way of
enjoying this relief: the* Via Ferrata, *an
itinerary combining hiking and rock-
climbing with all the necessary facilities.
Even though you need not drive your own
pitons and nuts into the crevices, there is
nothing easy about this trail. You will set
off to climb great cliffs, swivel a ladder over
the void, cross precipices several dozen
metres deep over a metal gangway with just
enough room for both feet together or else
clutching the two ropes dangling from
above. This should give you a better idea
of the delights and challenges facing you
on the* Via Ferrata *of La Colmiane, rated
"difficult but accessible to everyone". It is
also the oldest in the département.*

THE TINÉE VALLEY:
the sporting valley

1 *The Tinée river, 75 km long, has its source at Cime de la Bonette, 2,600 m above sea level.*
The torrent sometimes causes devastating floods in the upper valley, which stretches along the Argentera mountain range.

2 *Saint-Étienne-de-Tinée is the chief town in the upper Tinée valley, 1,142 m above sea level. Formerly a crossroads for mule trails linking the Mediterranean coast and Northern Provence, the Dauphiné and the Piedmont, it was renowned for its market and fairs. It has a remarkably rich architectural heritage.*

It is reputed to be a record-breaker. True, the Tinée valley is not lacking in arguments, the most spectacular being, unquestionably, the highest road in Europe, unpadlocked by the spring thaw for an escapade over the Col de Restefond into the Ubaye valley and towards the Hautes-Alpes département. Climbing the 2,692 metres to the top of the pass is a fierce endurance test for amateur cyclists and a test of automobile drivers' nerves. Everyone can appreciate the heady intoxication of contemplating the grandiose curtains of mountains, and the respect they inspire for the flora and fauna perceived in their pristine innocence. Just a healthy hike away, Vens and its waterfall and bubbling basins harmonise with the finest, if not the largest, series of glacial lakes in a département

which boasts many: if its 300 lakes were combined into one, it would cover 650 hectares. The Tinée valley has no notable canyons, but one cannot have everything. It is, however, the realm of Alpine skiing, with the two major winter ski resorts of Auron and Isola 2000, which some aficionados, too pressed for time, prefer to reach by helicopter. From the air, they can discern villages that are invisible from the road. Indeed, those who remain on the valley floor experience a strange feeling of solitude. Only when you have driven halfway up the valley to Saint-Sauveur do you encounter the first signs of a town, with its steep streets trampled by the hoofs of herds of sheep chiming the mountains. Downstream, the river has fallen silent; no longer carrying logs felled in the

1 *Saint-Érige church in the hamlet of Auron is a 13th-century Romanesque chapel built on the site where the horse of Saint Érige, bishop of Gap, stopped on a major route between the Mediterranean coast and the Ubaye valley to the North. In the background, Las Donnas massif.*

forests of Clans for the shipbuilders of Genoa or Toulon. All passers-by can see are the tiny roads winding their way upward. Should they answer the call and attempt the ascent, every peak seems inexhaustible. Beginning with the approach to the village of La Tour, with the last surviving oil mill in the entire valley, a reminder of its prosperous olive-growing past. Its White Penitents' chapel is decorated with murals by two 15th-century painters from Nice. Restored thanks to the services of one of the heirs to their artistic tradition, the structure offers a refreshed view of this type of decoration, a rare patinated view of which can been seen at Chapelle Saint-Sébastien in Saint-Étienne-de-Tinée at the upper end of the stream. Although the Tinée valley has no monopoly on this art form, its painted chapels illustrate

1 *The former hamlet of Auron (1,600 m above sea level) in the upper Tinée valley boasts 25 ski lifts, artificial snow, a skiing school and 140 km of ski runs, making it a very popular winter ski resort.*

its broad range. Their murals replaced the excessively expensive furniture. Their style is naive in Roure, with its strikingly steep roofs and the only panel painting by Brea in the valley. In Roubion, they form "the most accomplished and most appealing example of this local art form with all the narrative verve of the artist's Provençal temperament." Although it has been accessible by road only since 1947, Ilonse was never completely isolated from the world. A famous Occitan troubadour, Raymond Féraud, was the son of a local lord of this village. But here the mystery of the origins of the body of a young woman unearthed during excavations has never been solved. Perhaps the restored mediaeval castle of Marie, on the other side of the river,

*Traditional houses in
the upper Tinée valley.*

1

1 *The Isola 2000 ski resort, inaugurated in 1972, offers 120 km of ski runs and access to the Mercantour National Park and Col de la Lombarde on the Italian border. On the upper left, the Malinvern (2,938 m).*

2 *Near the village of Isola (873 m above sea level) stands the magnificent 12th-century Romanesque church tower, 16 metres tall, the only remains of the Saint-Pierre church devastated by a flood in the 16th century and replaced in 1690 by the Baroque church in the village, also dedicated to Saint Peter.*

3 *Trout fisherman in the Chastillon valley*

4 *Picking chestnuts near Isola. Many villages in the département have an autumn chestnut festival, Isola and Berre in particular.*

The six hectares of the Marcel Kroenlein mountain Arboretum (1,200 m above sea level) bring together deciduous and coniferous trees growing at altitudes ranging from 900 and 1,600 m.

1 *Roure, a tiny village with 91 inhabitants built on a rocky spur 1,090 m above sea level, overlooks the Vionène torrent. Its chapel dedicated to Saint Sebastian and Saint Bernard is decorated with murals, includes the "Vices", painted by Andrea de Cella (16th century).*

*T*he Arboretum of Roure: This celebration of deciduous and coniferous trees in Roure is a just tribute to the origins of the village. The etymology of its name refers to the Provençal word for the red oak. The old folks still remember the ancient colossal Quercus, which, like the spirit of a druid, symbolised durability in the midst of the slate and wood-roofed centuries-old houses and barns with stone porches and foundations. Also Director of the prestigious Exotic Garden of Monaco, Marcel Kroenlein did not consider it demeaning to manage this mountain fastness, where larch stand side by side with chestnut trees, to work with other volunteers to create a site reserved for Alpine-Mediterranean biology and ecology. With a scientific committee, it is dedicated to the observation and study of trees in the mountain stages, as well as wild rose (20 of the 27 species known in France) and houseleek. The Arboretum pursues its mission and here, visitors can admire cedars from the Atlas mountains, Bosnian pine, North American oak and the Asian maple tree, among other specimens from all over the world brought together on the Arboretum's 6 hectares, but make sure not to tread on the more fragile plant varieties.

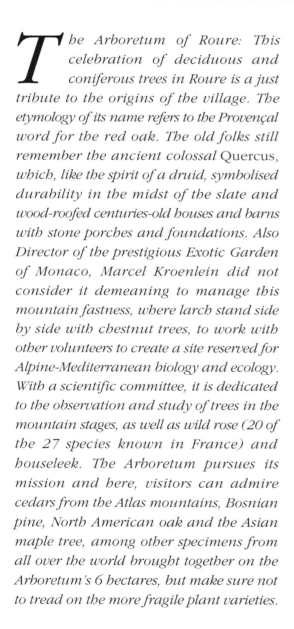

2 *Saint-Sauveur-sur-Tinée is built on a bend where the Tinée valley broadens at a crossroads favourable to social, religious and economic life. The partly Gothic (16th-century) church was rebuilt in the 17th century.*

3 *Rimplas stretches on a promontory 1,020 m above sea level between the Tinée valley and Vallon de Bramafan, against the backdrop of the snow-capped Pépoiri peak (2,674 m).*

4 *La Tour-sur-Tinée, built in tiers on a ridge projecting from the Tournairet massif, 640 m above sea level, has a beautiful Gothic church (15th century) decorated with murals painted in 1491 and houses with trompe-l'œil façades, illustrating influence from the Piedmont.*

① *The road from the splendid village of Ilonse, 1,190 m above sea level, to the main highway on the valley floor was opened just a half century ago. Chapelle Saint-Grat was built in the 17th century. In the background, the Gélas culminates at an altitude of 3,143 m.*

may remember who participated in the cavalcades down the Roman way through Val de Blore to Cimiez or Glandèves (Entrevaux). At the foot of its ski resort, with the highest golf course in Europe - the 18th in the département - Isola roasts its chestnuts in November, warming hands and hearts in the valley.

② *Bairols, a former fief of the Grimaldis of Beuil, stretches along the ridge of La Croix de Bairols along the old mule trail 860 m above sea level. In the background, the plateau of La Madone d'Utelle.*

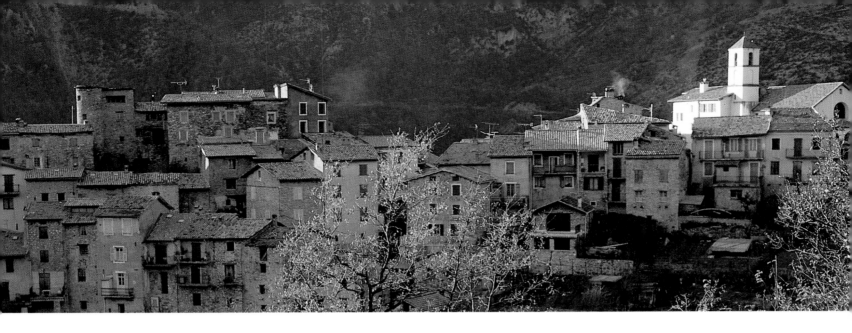

3 *The village of Marie, built 550 m above sea level on the gentle slope of a rocky spur in the midst of olive trees, turns its back on the Tinée river. Its tall houses built of dark stone perfectly illustrate the transition between Mediterranean and Alpine architecture. The church was built in the 17th century.*

4 *Above Roubion, a village stretching on a ridge 1,336 m above sea level at the foot of rocky overhangs, stands Chapelle Saint-Sébastien painted in 1513 by an unknown itinerant artist. The village has preserved remains of its fortifications and castle.*

THE VAR VALLEY:
a valley of many faces

Hooked by a fisherman in Entraunes, the trout is unaware that the cruel waters where it had made its home flow turbulently down to an Ornithological Reserve at the river's mouth, some 135 kilometres further South. The Var river is the link between the fish splashing at the foot of the larch trees near its source to the feathered creatures seeking refuge on the water rushing between the second largest airport in France and one of the main shopping centres on the Mediterranean coast. It is more than the département's main watercourse; it is the tie between the coast and the mountain hinterland, the people of the sea and those of the highlands, the web of history and the serpentine patchwork of the maritime Alps. At the end of its course, it is debonair and citified,

1 *The Var, 135 km long, with its 1.5 billion cubic metres yearly flow, the 2,822 km² drainage basin, is the region's largest river system. It has its source at the foot of Col de la Cayolle, 1,780 m above sea level, and its tributaries include the Roudoule, Cians, Tinée, Vésubie and Estéron rivers. At Plan du Var, the confluence of the Estéron and Var rivers opens onto the lower Var valley.*

2 *National Highway 202 is very familiar to skiers and hikers. The road follows the Var from its mouth up to Entrevaux, the main access route to the Estéron, Vésubie and Tinée valleys, and the Cians, Roudoule and Daluis gorges.*

3 *Fountain in La Roquette-sur-Var Fountains used to be key elements in protecting and structuring rural life, privileged meeting places for reinforcing solidarity among villagers.*

4 *La Roquette-sur-Var dominates the entire lower Var valley. In 1200, "Rochetta" protected a ford across the Var. The village changed lords many times in its history, belonging to the Béranger family in the 13th century, then successively to the Ranulfi, Litti, Lascaris and Grimaldis. In 1867 it lost nearly 500 ha of its territory with the creation of the new commune of Saint-Martin-du-Var.*

1

caught between glass towers. But, lest it be forgotten, at the slightest pretext, it returns to its primitive nature, a rampaging wild ram, its waters gushing out of its bed of pebbles, usually far too grand for the modest stream. Open to the cold wind blowing down from the snow-capped peaks, with its biting cold on winter mornings, in summer its corridor disperses the fragrances of the market gardens greening its banks to perfume the picturesque outdoor markets. Like its more illustrious northern models, its sun-baked hillsides display the very last vineyards of Saint-Roman-de-Bellet and Villars-sur-Var. Welcoming enterprises in search of level ground, the lower Var valley, once a rampart and a

1 *Carros: the perched site has preserved traces of prehistoric, Roman and Merovingian occupation. The village had a succession of lords until the 17th century, including the Blacas, Giraud and Ronciglioni families.*

2 *Villars-sur-Var. The population moved down from the Ligurian site on the hilltop of Saint-Jean to the fertile terrace below in the 1st century. "Vilario" lived through a succession of lords, wars, fires, epidemics until 1860 when it became French. Famous for its vineyards since the Middle Ages, today it produces the only "Côtes de Provence" AOC wine in the département.*

2

[3] *Gattières unfurls its six parallel streets on the hilltop at an altitude of 270 m above sea level. It overlooks a famous ford in the lower Var valley, already known to the Ligurians and Romans. The village belonged to the Entrevennes, the Count of Savoy in 1388, then the Grimaldis in 1390, the Dal Pozzo family in the 18th century and finally was handed over to France in 1760.*

border, now beats like a vital artery. Although it is never navigable, it offers its banks and even its bed for people to worm their way through the narrow Mescla gorges along the Route de Grenoble. There, joined by the waters of the Tinée and Vésubie rivers carrying moss and gentian from the uplands under more transparent skies, it becomes almost impulsive. Its meanders dialogue with the narrow-gauge railway, *"Le Train des Pignes"*, whose nickname evokes both pinecones and a local sweet. The century-old little train slowly wends its way up the river to sniff the lavender all the way to Digne, its wheels almost on the water, omitting no stops: Malaussène where the bandit Gaspard de Besse is said to have melted down the gold of his booty, Villars and its white wine famous since the

*Touët-sur-Var offers a striking appearance with its compact outer row of tall houses,
their attics gaping open towards the South and its church clinging to the bluff
overlooking the river. Once the property of the Templars, the Grimaldis of Beuil
and the Clarettis, it was occupied by French Revolutionary troops in 1793.
Below the village, highway RN 202 was built in 1863 and the narrow-gauge railway
between Nice and Digne in 1892.*

1

Middle Ages, Touët-sur-Var clinging to the cliffside with its little Romanesque church built over a waterfall, Puget-Théniers where the robust female nude sculptor Maillol's fashioned in tribute to the Revolutionary figure, Louis-Auguste Blanqui, no longer raises Puritan hackles... At this crossroads for sheep-raising surrounded by rich orchards, the fan-shaped cleft excavated by the Roudoule river remains a geological curiosity. By a sort of miracle due to the will of a few individuals, life has not deserted this little valley, in spite of closing down copper mines; the département's first "ecomuseum" describes their joys and sorrows. Then the Var River becomes a sharp blade cutting through the prune-coloured shale of the Gorges of Daluis. As for the parallel gash in the Cians valley, these

1 The winter ski resort of Valberg opened in 1930 at the instigation of Count Victor de Cessole who, starting in 1909, contributed to popularising skiing, particularly in the Mercantour mountains. The 27th French Ski Championship in 1938 put the Alpes-Maritimes resorts on the map. Today, Valberg is one of the French Riviera's four best-equipped winter resorts, with a wide range of ski lifts, a ski club and a skiing school.

canyons are striking in their deep purple garb. In Guillaumes, shepherds' tales rise along the ridges black with conifers to the dismantled castle. In the midst of its mountain pasture, the first to be taken over by the joys of skiing, Beuil is indissociably linked to the memory of its lords, the most turbulent in the region, the Grimaldis. We can imagine their cavalcades through the Val d'Entraunes when the poplar trees weep their gold on past grandeur.

2 *Valberg in summer. After a century of semi-somnolence, summer tourism is thriving again in the region, boosted by Alpinism, hiking, rock-climbing, paragliding, mountain biking and riding, which together offer a new approach to the mountains.*

1 The castle of Guillaumes was built in 1450 by King René, Count of Provence, and the village became a key stronghold on the border with the Comté de Nice. A permanent garrison was posted there by French King Henri IV in 1575. The famous military engineer Vauban updated the castle and reinforced the town ramparts at the end of the 17th century. When Guillaumes was given to the Kingdom of Sardinia in 1760 in exchange for several other villages, the fortifications were dismantled.

2 The trompe-l'œil façade of the town hall in Guillaumes.

3 "La Tête de Femme" (woman's head), a natural rock formation at the entrance to the Gorges of Daluis on the road up to Guillaumes.

HOTEL de VILLE
1998

4 In the Gorges of Daluis, the Var flows under "Pont de la Mariée" (bride's bridge), built for the former tramway to Guillaumes that operated from 1922 to 1928. Today, it is a popular site for rafting and bungee jumping.

1 2 *Entraunes, Saint-Martin, Villeneuve and Châteauneuf-d'Entraunes formed an isolated land, their inhabitants living in virtually total independence until 1700. The Romanesque church in Saint-Martin houses a famous panel painting, the Virgin of the Rosary by François Brea (1555). The village of Villeneuve d'Entraunes is built against the rocky ridge of La Maïre.*

3 *Col de la Cayolle: access to the pass is along a narrow winding flower-lined road. At an altitude 2,000 metres above sea level, it is possible to spot marmots and snow hares among the pine trees tortured by the winds.*

154

The works to build the "Train des Pignes" (the pinecone train, so slow it was possible to pick up pinecones along the track) began in 1902. In all, it took no less than 25 tunnels, 16 viaducts and 15 metal bridges for this line 150 km long. Since World War I, the line has been regularly threatened with being closed down, but it has survived so far, even after the natural disaster that caused serious damage requiring large-scale repairs in 1996. The steam engine inaugurated in 1980 on part of the line gave the train a major boost. The train stops in all the villages along the Var, before pursuing its course through grandiose landscapes on its way to Saint-André-les-Alpes via Annot, Le Fugeret, Méailles and Thorame.

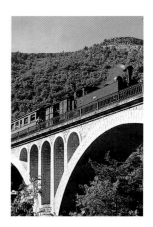

*E*comusée de la Roudoule. *Once upon a time, there was a dying valley. Then, as happens in sagas, the four Maurin brothers rushed in. Born in Puget-Rostang, where they had left their parents without abandoning their roots, they were saddened one spring day to see hope waning as time went by. Another spring day, they brought their youth and circle of friends to instil new life into the valley. Puget-Rostang, Auvare, Saint-Léger, La Croix-sur-Roudoule and Rigaud have seen their colours restored, along with daily activity, noise and old-fashioned solidarity. The villages have come together around the "Ecomuseum", a beacon shedding light on the past and marking out the future. It provides visitors and urban schoolchildren with moving evocations of the past, frozen like the surprising geological and mining heritage. Slaughtering the hog in winter, distilling lavender and threshing grain, picking mushrooms in autumn, all become vibrant lessons on life and nature, which also help better understand our own selves. In a land where painters travelled from village to village leaving masterpieces in their wake, the sculptor Ange Maurin, who started it all, carves olive wood and dreams on: what if his end of the world were to become another world, with neither merchandise nor artifice.*

The Roudoule river cuts through 250 million years of history. The Écomusée de la Roudoule *has set up nature trails to discover the flora, forests and geology. Copper was mined in Léouvé until 1886.*

1 *Rigaud between the lower and upper Gorges of the Cians, 700 m above sea level. The village has an Alpine character with its houses topped by the characteristic attics for drying fruit and grain. It belonged to the Knights Templar in the 12th and 13th centuries.*

2 *Puget-Théniers, with a proto-historic Ligurian occupation, became Roman in 49 BC, Provençal in the 11th century, went to the House of Savoy in 1348. Its lords were the Grimaldis of Beuil in the 16th century and the town became a sub-Prefecture under French rule. In the 19th century, it had tanneries and hat and cloth factories. Highway RN 202 in 1879 and the railway in 1892 made Puget-Théniers a hub for all the roads from the coast, upper Provence, the Dauphiné and Piémont.*

3 *Puget-Rostang, in 1252, the fief of the Rostaing de Thorame, who left it their name. The village, 700 m above sea level, is dominated by its former castle keep.*

THE ESTÉRON VALLEY: a valley out of time

Of the main valleys of the hinterland, the Estéron is the closest to the coast. Yet it is the most distinctive, the most secretive, as if it had been forgotten. So much so, that some maps even hesitate to mention the road following its course. And those who have found it may wonder where they are headed. Unlike the other valleys, which do not disdain the celebrity of winter or summer resorts in their uppermost reaches, the Estéron retains the mystery of its finiteness. You don't work your way up the valley to go somewhere, even though it is said to connect with the Verdon valley. This valley is not a trail and has no use for such functionality. It beckons no one and remains aloof. As soon as you have crossed the bridge over the Var, you are misled with the connivance of the village of Bonson. With the micaceous glitter of its olive trees,

1 Roquestéron is divided in two. After 1388, one half was in Provence, the other in Savoy, and in 1860, while both became French, they remained separate communes, with the largest, Roquestéron-Puget, the "capital" of the Estéron valley.

2 Roquestéron-Grasse, the original nucleus of the settlement, is a fortified village at the foot of the spur topped by the Romanesque Sainte-Pétronille chapel with its sober charm.

3 Pierrefeu, "Petrofocus" mentioned in the 11th century, was founded as a Roman outpost watching over the Var and Estéron valleys. The V-shaped village is built around two sheer peaks overlooking the waters of the Riou de Pierrefeu.

4 Gilette, built on a rocky spur topped by the castle of the Counts of Provence (12th/13th centuries), dominates the mouth of the Estéron river. Between the mountain and the spur, on either side of the pass, a bridge connects the two parts of the village. Below, the Estéron's waters flow into the Var.

the village draws and diverts attention northward. This is not really the wrong track, but the Estéron has, at least temporarily, succeeded in dodging intruders. Facing West, it remains huddled between the great limestone mass of the Cheiron to the South and Gourdan and Mont-Vial peaks to the North, towering from their height of 1,500 metres over this gateway to the invisible. The most obstinate will manage in the end to find the river's trace, but beware! it wriggles like a glistening eel in the rocky folds closing behind it, like so many portcullises, its narrow gorges, or *clues*: Cerise, Riolan, Mujols and Aiglun, one of the finest in upper Provence. The most aventuresome let themselves slide through their waters, for a better view from below of the pristine wilderness on the slopes dotted with broom from which they may spy a wild boar pursued

1 *Caille, a small village mentioned under the name "Calia" in 1042, stretches along the road in the middle of the immense grassy Plateau des Sagnes.*

2 *The Estéron has its source near Soleilhas, 1,130 m above sea level. After flowing 65 km between the Cheiron massif and the mountains of Bleyne, Thorenc and Charamel, its waters join those of the Var.*

3 *Sigale, perched on a ridge 630 m above sea level, overlooks the Estéron and Riolan valleys. Just 3 km east of the village, the chapel of Notre-Dame d'Entrevignes is decorated with murals painted in 1536.*

1 *Saint-Auban: overlooking the village, 1,100 m above sea level, stand the ruins of the castle keep and old village rampart built on the top of the ridge in the 13th century. To the east of the village, the spectacular vertiginous walls of the Clue de Saint-Auban.*

by a pack of hunting dogs. And with a little luck, they may see a few rooftops seeming to try to go unnoticed: Sigale, Le Mas, Sallagriffon, Collongues or Les Mujouls. As long as they are humble and frugal - qualities that are hardly modern - people are tolerated by the stones that may even provide refuge, as in Cuébris. The old church of Pierrefeu is the ideal home for the *"Musée hors du temps"* (Museum out of time). The Estéron valley remains indifferent to the world. It was not always so timeless when it prolonged the international border along the Var. There milestones still stand, bearing the French fleur-de-lis and the Cross of Savoy, like scars on torn skin between Provence and the Comté de Nice, between the Kingdom of France and the Holy Roman Empire. Overlooking the confluence with the Var, Gilette is proud of its hanging fountain,

*I*s Clue de Riolan, as claimed by some, the most beautiful itinerary in a département that, without exaggerating, boasts some of the most remarkable clues *and canyons in Europe? Cutting its serrate notch several hundred metres below limestone walls before its confluence with the Estéron, the Riolan torrent exhausts the limbs and satisfies the eyes of those brave enough to follow its course. A tiny torrent for monumental thrills: four hours of floating through an impetuous maze of stone blocks, jumping heights of several metres, passing under seeping rocks with only your mouth out of the water, sliding down toboggans, roping up waterfalls. As with the thirty some marked courses along streams (Maglia, Bendola, Amen, Raton, Peïra, Gourgas, etc.) and many other white-water sports, such activities require thorough preparation and all the right precautions. The grandeur of these sites does not preclude prudence and the intoxication of the sport is no dispensation from respecting the flora and fauna, even when they remain invisible.*

1 *Thorenc is a residential hamlet 1,250 m above sea level, which became a popular health resort at the end of the 19th century. There is still a sanatorium run by the French clergy* (Clergé de France), *a 19th-century castle and the ruins of the former village with its fortress and chapel.*

2 *Gars, mentioned in 1158, was granted in 1383 to Pierre de Terminis by the Count of Provence, then burned in 1400 by the Grimaldis of Beuil. The village is huddled at the foot of the Montagne de Gars (1 192 m).*

3 *Briançonnet, founded by the ancient Romans, displays traces of its role as a commercial crossroads back in the 3rd century. The 12th-century Romanesque church houses a panel painting of the Virgin, attributed to Louis Brea.*

4 *Aiglun enjoyed a time of great prosperity in the 13th century. The village became French in 1760. Its Provençal architecture displays alpine influences with its tall houses topped by an open attic for drying fruit and grain.*

5 *The alpine environment of Thorenc with its splendid prairies and pine forests in an exceptionally sunny microclimate.*

even more so of its castle, the site of a famous battle during the French Revolution, immortalised by a painting in the Gallery of Battles in the Château de Versailles. Further upstream, Roquestéron, split in two by history, its halves staring each other in the eye from their respective banks of the river. It is hard to say whether Tourette-du-Château feels any nostalgia when evoking the fate of Annibal Grimaldi de Beuil, the last *condottiere* in this forgotten valley who, after betraying his suzerain, was executed in his castle, of which almost nothing remains.

THE MERCANTOUR PARK:
sacred heights

The Alpes-Maritimes is a land of history, far beyond the history written in manuals. Almost every artlessly taken step follows in those of a distant past pregnant with meaning. Within a radius of 50 kilometres around Nice, there is a remarkable concentration covering a million years of history: Vallonnet and Lazaret caves, Terra Amata. The artefacts unearthed are displayed in museums, some built on the very site of their discovery: tools, carvings, jewellery and even human skeletons, all remains that we cannot actually touch. But the most moving of these is not confined in walls. It is out in the open, windblown, like other ancient European spiritual centres: Brocéliande in Brittany, Stonehenge in Britain,

[1] *Early Bronze Age rock carvings in the Vallée des Merveilles (1,800-1,500 BC).*

[2] *The Gélas Massif (3,143 m), the highest point in the Alpes-Maritimes.*

[3] *The hamlet of Saint-Grat in the Gordolasque valley, covered with fine subalpine vegetation in summer.*

166

1 *High mountain landscape in autumn in the crystalline Mercantour massif.*

2 Tarantola mauritanica, *a gecko.*

Delphi in ancient Greece. The *Vallée des Merveilles* (Valley of Wonders), north of Monaco and Menton, is not easy to reach. After leaving Saint-Dalmas-de-Tende, a steep trail rises above the larch trees through the scree. "Higher still, the foothills curve their backbone like antediluvian monsters in a maze of galleries at the foot of the cliffs with their bronze or flame-coloured patina, verdigris slopes and polished slabs of stone glistening like shields. The mass of the ancient glaciers shaped this setting, whose strangeness constantly suggests the presence of unknown telluric forces crouching under the skin of the rock." Let us once again let the mountain poet Samivel speak: "Such a structure may strike any

visitor with its savage grandeur. But it also has an even rarer virtue, more subtle, the quality of the unusual, whose perspectives let us know confusedly that they are pursued beyond their own immediate appearance, harbouring a hidden treasure or mystery." On the exact origin and meaning of the 40,000 signs in this "mysterious treasure", engraved nearly four thousand years ago, discovered in the 17th century but not seriously studied until 1868, there are many divergent interpretations. Who were the peoples who gathered around the ridge of Mont Bego rumbling under the clouds? What did they seek to express in their clumsy geometric, human and animal shapes? Scientists can

③ *"Lambert" (green lizard)*

④ *Gialorgues lakes dominated by the impressive stratified sandstone bars supporting Cime Delfy and Fort Carra in the Mercantour National Park.*

A Reserve for life forms. The saxifrage blooms only once in its life of several decades and grows here like nowhere else. It comes directly from the Cenozoic Era. Although it is rooted in virtually inaccessible places it is threatened by Man, which is why it is specially protected. The Mercantour National Park originally selected the plant to be its emblem. Of the 20,000 plant species growing on its territory, 150 are rare and 32 endemic. This goes to show that the creation of the Park, though much disputed, was justified. It was also in keeping with the tradition of the Royal Hunting Grounds instituted in 1861 by order of King Emmanuel II of Italy with the same environmental - and cynegetic - concern (which entails no contradiction). There are 158 protected animal species in the Park, including 600 chamois and 350 ibex, 1,200 mouflon, some thirty pairs of golden eagles, a few peregrine falcons and... 19 species of bats the poet Jacques Audiberti referred to with the colourful Provençal term, rate penado *(winged mouse). And there are newcomers: the bearded vulture brought in by Man in 1992 and, a little later, the wolf, which no one seemed to expect. Nature is more imaginative than humans who, whether shepherd or hunter, will have to invent the right sort of coexistence in this Reserve.*

1 *Flora and fauna in the Mercantour massif, with ibex, chamois, mouflon, marmot, horned owls, etc.*

2 *Cows at* Lac des Grenouilles *(Frog lake) in the valley of Fontanalbe. It takes four hours to hike around the Mercantour's glacial lakes in the midst of subalpine flora (rhododendron, artemisia, edelweiss, columbine, saxifrage, marginated primrose...).*

3 *Horses in the upper valley of Mollières - Caïre and Cime de Rogué.*

1 *Snow on* Lac du Boréon
(1,500 m above sea level).
In summer, this is a meeting
place for rock-climbers and
hikers in the Mercantour Park.

2 *Shore of* lacs de Morgon
with its grassy snow-covered
knolls; in the distance,
Pas de la Cavale.

3 *The large* Lac de Vens *is*
one of six lakes in the Upper
Tinée valley, 600 m long
and 2,327 m above sea level.

ramble on infinitely, as the uninitiated smile on. To those in search of a reason or purpose, the stone remains as silent as the hollow marble gaze of Greek statues. Little is required to be "awe-struck": treading the thick grass and flowers between the "emerald" lakes, breathing in the wind that carries the magic of the rock it caresses, touching the lustral water bearing the reflection of one's eyes, abandoning oneself to the clouds as if they were divine messengers. Here, everything, including the chosen name, speaks of the sacred. Evil, too, with the demonic connotations of many recent names like *Cime du Diable* (Devil's Ridge) or *Val d'Enfer* (Valley of Hell). Inalterable, the soul of the world radiates in silence.

Upper Fenestre Valley

1 Corniculate petroglyph: "vandalised" stone

2 Cephalomorphic petroglyph: "Christ's stone".

3 Series of rock engravings in Vallée des Merveilles. The best known is the "Sorcerer", arms raised and brandishing two daggers. "Who were the peoples who gathered around the ridge of Mont Bego rumbling under the clouds? What did they seek to express in their clumsy geometric, human and animal shapes...?"

For two hundred years, the legend has been written every day. Yet everything contributes to bringing the present closer to the past. Perhaps the climate, the beaches, golf courses, exoticism... or the limpid, gentle life? The water is as blue in many other places. Not to mention there are other, more financial attractions. For tourism perhaps. But for pleasure? Here, only space is thrifty. "Stop, traveller!" said Henri Bosco, in an invitation to exploratory nonchalance. And stop counting. The treasure is in keeping with the measure of the senses to be titillated and the time to be spent. Indeed, few lands offer such a profusion of colour, fragrance, flavour, sounds and signs: all sorts of creations shaped by the hands of potters, glass-blowers, chefs, cabinet makers, stonemasons; melodic, pictorial, literary, poetic, philosophical works, some by spirits fulfilled, others uttered with the last creative breath. All laud the joyousness to the song of the "Mistral wind, wiping out the clouds and driving out melancholy." The wind, like art and influence, mocks the mountain peaks. And in the Middle Ages, reputedly so dark, this land, so inhospitable in appearance, was a crossroads from Lombardy, Piedmont, Provence and Catalonia. Artists past and present. In this land where everything is a pretext for celebration, however bizarre or insignificant (gourds in Nice or snails in Tourrette-Levens), Nature has its rightful place; it has laboured, gardened, staged. Man has assisted the gods. From stone, earth, raw materials, Man has drawn hues, raised forms. They inspire meditation, protect from the Evil Eye or exalt pride. They blend into their environment or stand out on the contrary. Provocative as they are nowhere else. Many trees come from faraway places, brought in by foreigners and local people (Jean-François Bermond, Antoine Risso): mimosa, agave, eucalyptus, palm trees, avocado, guava, datura altered the original landscapes. To play their part in the show, they were mixed in parks with classical lines and jungles of Romantic inspiration. Reverie, nostalgia in the gardens of the cloister in Cimiez. Every year, these mineral or leafy settings host a thousand and one festivities: classical music on the starry parvis of Saint-Michel in Menton, Le Suquet or the courtyard of the Princely Palace in Monaco, jazz in the olive grove of Cimiez or the pine grove of Juan-les-Pins, painting in the castles of Cagnes-sur-Mer, Villeneuve-Loubet, Antibes, Vallauris and dozens of other museums. The largest number in Europe dedicated to modern art. Opera in Nice and Monte Carlo, ballet, symphonic music, theatre and theatre cafés, schools of dance and music, all maintain a tradition of quality that goes back to the Belle Epoque. When the Riviera made and unmade reputations. "Successfully introducing and performing meant certain popularity in ten foreign capitals." Wagner's *Lohengrin* was performed here in 1881, six years before Paris, his *Parsifal* thirty years before. For those who travel, there is no site, no district, no street, that does not echo a work, reveal the shadow of a guest, dissimulate a secret love whose heroes are part of yesterday and today's history: King Leopold of Belgium, Jean Cocteau, Napoleon Bonaparte, the Aga Khan, Isadora Duncan, Pablo Picasso, Grace Kelly. The air is filled with particles of talent, toil and slices of life, both modest and famous. Those who breathe it are indeed fortunate.

THE HUMAN FACTOR
The sea, mountains and heritage of the French Riviera

Nice - Church of
the Franciscan convent
of Cimiez: altarpiece of the
Crucifixion by Ludovic Brea.

1 The altarpiece includes
portraits of David and Isaiah
in the corners and
a predella illustrating four
episodes of Christ's Passion
including the bearing
of the Cross.

2 On the right, two
enigmatic figures absorbed
in conversation, seem
oblivious to the scene.

3 A major work by
Ludovic Brea (dated 1512),
the retable of the Crucifixion
features Christ's final
moments with theatrical
staging. Alongside
the traditional figures
(the Virgin Mary, Saint John
and Saint Mary-Magdalene),
the painter has included
Saint Francis of Assisi
bearing the stigmata and
Saint Jerome beating
his breast with a stone.

LAND OF RELIGION: religious fervour, secular exuberance

With the song of the cicadas and the sunshine in the sweltering heat, towns and villages come alive each in turn, like lights on a summer firtree. Summer is the time of votive feasts, or f*estins*. For one day at least, communities extend their hospitality to amazed strangers, reinforcing their solidarity around their patron saint and the tangible features of their faith: mass and local fair, chorale and dance, communion and feasting. Between the church and town hall, the plane trees conspire in a blend of religious fervour and secular exuberance. Such connivance is ancestral. The issues of the world above in no way overshadow the more down-to-earth joy of being together; nor does piety dampen volubility. Otherwise, the Carnival of Nice, which never denied its

The range of façades
on religious structures
reflects the diversity
of periods in history and
expressions of Faith.

⬚1 At L'Escarène, the three
17th-century façades of
the parish church flanked
by the two Penitents' chapels
present a monumental
alignment.

⬚2 The former Cathedral
of Grasse.

⬚3 The fortified monastery
of Lérins is a fine example
of Romanesque architecture.

⬚4 The surprising
Notre-Dame-Auxiliatrice
church, built of concrete
in the 1930s by the Salesian
order, is splendidly decorated.

⬚5 The curved façade and
portico of the church
of the former Abbey of
Saint-Pons in Nice.

⬚6 The polychrome façade
of Saint Nicholas' Russian
Orthodox Cathedral.

⬚7 The calade (mosaic
of pebbles) on the parvis
in front of Saint-Michel
church in Menton.

distant pagan ancestry in the Roman Saturnalia, would never have survived the Middle Ages or chaste ecclesiastical reprimand, to become the "world's most famous" in the Belle Époque. In the winter chill, the harbinger of Spring and its flowers - we would like to see unaffected by the insults of time - drew "his burlesque or bucolic scaffolding peopled with captive creatures like organdie bees in their artificial paradise." When, from the cortège of grotesque papier-mâché figures there emerged an almost diabolical representation, like the *Ratapignata* ("bat" in *Nissard*), it recalled the sometimes ribald escapades of Satan, a source of many of the fireside story-telling in the valleys above. The image of the malevolent Tempter surrounded by his court is far more frightening when

184

Steeples punctuate
the landscape, striking
markers on the urban scene.
Several Romanesque
structures can be seen in
the upper mountain valleys
with their pyramidal roofs.

☐1 Saint-Dalmas-Valdeblore.

☐2 La Brigue.

☐3 Baroque models were often
applied in the construction
and reconstruction of
churches in urban centres.
Such is the case of
Saint-Jacques (Saint James')
church in Old Nice,
better known as Sainte-Rita.

☐6 Or Saint-Michel church in
Menton.

adorning bas-reliefs in the innumerable churches and
chapels scattered among the peaks and valleys of the
land. Nearly five hundred have been inventoried, built
over a period of four centuries starting in the late
Middle Ages, differing as much in their majesty as in
their location. The faith that built these sanctuaries and
motivated the artists who decorated them was
boundless. In terms of religious devotion, the tiniest
villages were as enterprising as bustling towns.
The distribution of the most sublime panel paintings
by Brea and other regional painters reveals no
hierarchy. Some of the most eloquent examples include
Sainte-Réparate Cathedral in Nice and the churches
dedicated to Saint Michael in Menton and Sospel. But
modest villages, like Venanson with its Saint-Sébastien

chapel, a jewel of Gothic art, Clans with its Romanesque Sainte-Marie collegiate church and the hamlet of Auron, whose famous chapel was chosen by the winged horse of Saint-Erige according to legend. In L'Escarène, Saint-Pierre and the two Penitents' chapels flanking it form a remarkable complex. From Notre-Dame-de-l'Assomption in Puget-Théniers to Santa Maria in Albis in Breil or Saint-Martin in La Brigue, the list seems endless. Strangely enough, many of these treasures are far off the beaten track. In times past, they often occupied places of immemorial faith, near a peak or a spring, and provided refuge to exhausted travellers or peasants caught in a storm. Places of worship for contemplation, propitiatory monuments against the scourges of this world, their isolation highlights the

4 *The entrance and church tower of the Abbey of Lérins.*

5 *Modern architecture has devised more daring shapes: here Sainte-Jeanne d'Arc (Saint Joan of Arc) church in Nice.*

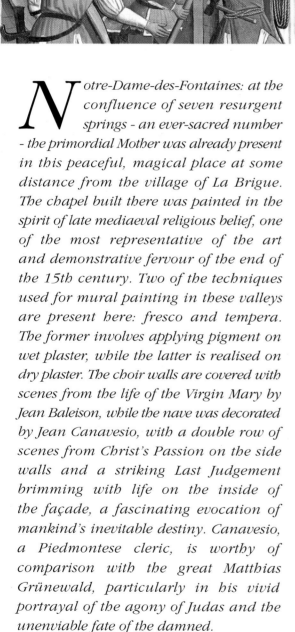

*N*otre-Dame-des-Fontaines: at the confluence of seven resurgent springs - an ever-sacred number - the primordial Mother was already present in this peaceful, magical place at some distance from the village of La Brigue. The chapel built there was painted in the spirit of late mediaeval religious belief, one of the most representative of the art and demonstrative fervour of the end of the 15th century. Two of the techniques used for mural painting in these valleys are present here: fresco and tempera. The former involves applying pigment on wet plaster, while the latter is realised on dry plaster. The choir walls are covered with scenes from the life of the Virgin Mary by Jean Baleison, while the nave was decorated by Jean Canavesio, with a double row of scenes from Christ's Passion on the side walls and a striking Last Judgement brimming with life on the inside of the façade, a fascinating evocation of mankind's inevitable destiny. Canavesio, a Piedmontese cleric, is worthy of comparison with the great Matthias Grünewald, particularly in his vivid portrayal of the agony of Judas and the unenviable fate of the damned.

1 *The interior of these structures often bears striking painted decoration, from small rural chapels like Saint-Sébastien in Roubion to such complex architectural masterpieces as the Chapelle de la Miséricorde in Nice, with their vaults covered with fine murals.*

2 *The rich interior of Saint-Michel church in Menton includes splendid Damascene velvet wall hangings offered by Honoré II, the first Prince of Monaco.*

3 *Decorative motifs from all over the world can be found in religious structures devoted to other faiths, as seen here in Saint George's, the Anglican church in Cannes.*

1

2

3

strong contrast between their bare exterior and the splendour of their interior. Sometimes with neither porch nor apse, they look more like a sheepfold with a 360° "illustrated catechism". On their walls, the likes of Canavesio, Baleison, Andrea de Cella and many other, anonymous, artists worked with tempera or *fresco* to paint biblical scenes and moral precepts that remain as edifying as ever for sinners. The Last Judgement at Notre-Dame-des-Fontaines inspired Maurice Toesca with a comparison to Brueghel. More recently, other artists, like Picasso, Matisse, Bellini or Cocteau renewed this tradition of painted chapels.

1

RIVIERA OF THE ARTS: a great art studio

Not everyone has yielded to the fascination. But, for over a century, many writers, painters, filmmakers, musicians, dancers from northern climes travelled South to catch a whiff of the ambience. And they all found their Holy Grail: kinship with his native Crete for Nikos Kazantzakis in search of "Asceticism" in Old Antibes; amorous and alcoholic exhilaration for F. Scott and Zelda Fitzgerald surrounded by a colony of rich idle Americans and authors such as Hemingway, Dos Passos and Gertrude Stein, just to name a few. For the French writer Paul Valéry it was "every atom of silence" and the German philosopher Nietzsche was amazed by the "exceptional dryness of the air" and was "convinced that under such a sky [he could] work on what he considered to be the hardest and most

1 *Count Tolstoy painted
by E. Répine in 1888.
His mystic dissident writing
made him the idol
of young 19th-century
Russians. Leo Tolstoy wrote*
The Cossacks *in Nice.*

overwhelming piece of work any human being would ever dream of." The sky was loyal to him and never let him down during his transmutation of values. Monet spent some time in the Spring of 1887 at La Garoupe where he discovered a new magic world of soft shades of pink and blue. Nice was a source of inspiration for many: Meyerbeer, Glinka and Verdi composed many of their most beautiful masterpieces there, Empress Eugénie danced to the music of Offenbach and Paganini played his violin here for the last time. This is where Tolstoy wrote *The Cossacks* and Jules Verne prepared a theatrical adaptation of *Around the world in 80 days*. Meissonnier and van Dongen painted in Cannes, Soutine and Derain came to Cagnes-sur-Mer just a few years apart. Some visitors were more like migrant birds,

Italian composer Giuseppe Verdi
(Roncole 1813 - Milan 1901)
wrote some of his music in Nice.

Collège de France *professor Paul Valéry*
(Sète 1871 - Paris 1945)
gave lectures in Nice.

German composer
Giacomo Meyerbeer
(Berlin 1791 - Paris 1864).

German composer, (naturalised French),
Jacques Offenbach
(Cologne 1819 - Paris 1880).

Painter Henri Matisse (Le Cateau-Cambrésis 1869 - Nice 1954)
was also a sculptor as can be seen here.

The photographer
photographed:
André Villers in
his garden, surrounded
by his pictures of artists.

The painter, engraver and
decorator Marc Chagall
(Vitebsk 1887 -
Saint-Paul-de-Vence 1985)
photographed in front of
his museum in Nice in 1970.

hovering between two periods, two havens. Nabokov took advantage of a stopover to pen his last books in Russian before crossing the Atlantic. Paul Gadenne completed his very last book in 1955 in Vence, where D.H. Lawrence and Albert Paraz chose to die. Others met here by chance, like Apollinaire, Kessel and Henry Miller, who was a judge at the Cannes Film Festival. Together with him, Louis Nucera discovered the joys of cycling. Some actually came against their will: Léger had sworn he would never set foot in the Midi, where "there was too much sun". The sun didn't hold it against him and he has his museum in Biot, while Chagall has his in Nice. Renoir, who died before Bonnard who spent his last days in Le Cannet, had barely closed his eyes for the last time amid the olive trees in Les Collettes

1 *The Spanish painter, draughtsman, engraver and sculptor Pablo Picasso (Malaga 1881 - Mougins 1973) in an impersonation of the famous criminal Landru.*

2 *The architect, urban planner, theorist and painter Edouard Le Corbusier (La Chaux-de-Fonds 1887 - Roquebrune-Cap-Martin 1965).*

3 *The painter Fernand Léger (Argentan 1881 - Gif-sur-Yvette 1955) seated in front of* Mas Saint-André *in Biot in 1954. After his death, his home became a museum, raised to the rank of National museum in 1967.*

4 *Pablo Picasso and Jean Cocteau at the opening of an exhibition in Mougins in 1956.*

5 *The painter and photographer Hans Hartung (Leipzig 1904 - Antibes 1989) with his companion Eva Bergman in their home and studio in Antibes in 1974.*

when Matisse decided to settle in Nice. A few years later, Picasso began hopping around from Antibes to Vallauris, then Juan-les-Pins, Cannes and finally Mougins, where he stayed until the end of his life. This "Bed of Camellias" laid the cornerstone for what would in the 60s become the incorrectly christened "School of Nice". This term was coined purely for convenience sake, according to Arman, whose name is associated with those of Yves Klein, Martial Raysse and César. But the history of contemporary art "would have taken a completely different turn, had it not been for all these activities and meetings in the region of Nice," according to the first appointed Director of the Centre Pompidou. In 1910, the *Ballets Russes* made a first appearance in Monte Carlo and, for the next 30 years, the Principality was recognised worldwide as the reference

③ The sculptor César (Marseille 1921 - Paris 1998) had lived in the region since 1960 (first a house in Roquefort-les-Pins, a flat in Old Nice, then hotel rooms or friends' homes) and often worked in Nice in the studios of friends like Soardi, Vernassa and Ossona, in constant search of new sources of inspiration and new friends. He has left us, among other things, his many compressions of automobiles and objects of all sorts, his "Thumb" and the "César" statuette for the French cinema awards. He can be seen, on page 199, in his favourite places, with his friends Colette and Jean-Pierre Soardi, working in their studio, leaning against one of his works or cooking his famous pasta.

① *Sacha Sosno (with Arman) seated at the foot of one of his sculptures,* Il faut en toute chose préférer l'intérieur à l'extérieur *(In all things it is best to prefer the inside to the outside), a bronze Venus embedded in marble of Carrara near Acropolis.*

② *Since 1950, first in his 'Laboratoire 32", where he organised jumble sales of used goods, his own works and those of others, Ben has been playing the clown and* agent provocateur *on the scene of Nice, to which he has remained ever faithful. He has just inaugurated "the centre of the World", a meeting place for artists, with creations by Ben as well as both the younger and older generations.*

for choreographic innovation. Diaghilev and Nijinsky had the genius to bring together music, painting and the visual arts in performances with music by Rimsky Korsakov, Georges Poulenc, Georges Auric, Darius Milhaud, Manuel de Falla or Maurice Ravel, stage sets by Juan Gris, Max Ernst, Joan Miró, Marie Laurencin, Chirico, Utrillo, Braque, Masson or Lurçat and even a scenario by Jean Cocteau with costumes by Coco Chanel. Somerset Maugham fled the mists of his homeland for the *Villa Mauresque* in Saint-Jean-Cap-Ferrat,

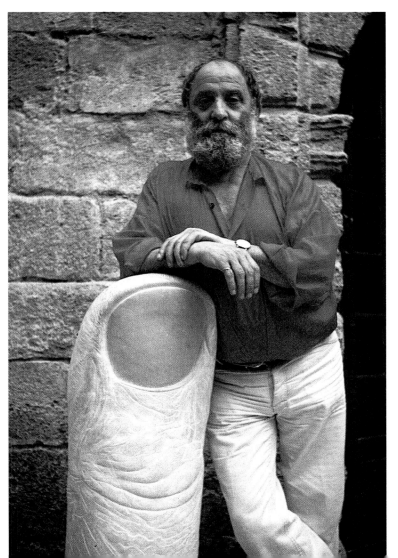

*T*he glassworks of Biot: abandoned in the late 19th century, glass blowing was revived and developed into a thriving art form in the 1950s. A potter by trade, Éloi Monod invented rustic bubble glass by adding sodium carbonate to the paste during the blowing process. Today Biot is a crossroads of the art of glass making with the Verrerie, at the foot of the village, both a beacon of creativity and a cosmopolitan showcase. In the workshop, the molten matter is folded before the visitors' eyes according to utilitarian or decorative purposes of Mephistophelian Hades, of which some, like Novaro and Zoritchak, have become eminent masters. A short distance away, a building with large bay windows, Galerie Internationale du Verre, hosts Les Verriales, which soon became an artistic showcase, virtually unique in France. Systematically enhancing creativity in the fashioning of glass in all its forms, each year this event presents major works both in terms of their artistic value as for their size and technical prowess.

1 *Sculptures by Germaine Richier on the terrace of the Picasso museum of Antibes.*

2 *Entrance to the* Musée Départemental des Merveilles *in Tende.*

3 *The Miró labyrinth at the Fondation Maeght in Saint-Paul.*

4 *Façade of the Léger museum in Biot, inaugurated in 1960.*

5 *The Ephrussi de Rothschild museum in Saint-Jean-Cap-Ferrat is a genuine treasure-trove.*

6 *The Villa Kerylos in Beaulieu is an evocation of an ancient Greek home.*

7 *The Museum of History and Archaeology of Antibes.*

8 *The MAMAC (Museum of Modern and Contemporary Art) in Nice.*

9 *The grand staircase in Palais Lascaris, Old Nice.*

10 *The Musée de la Castre, Le Suquet, Cannes.*

11 *Villa Arson, National Contemporary Art Centre in Nice.*

12 *Façade of the Matisse Museum and its exceptional collection of works, furniture and objects, retracing the life of Henri Matisse, probably the artist who has best expressed and exalted our region.*

where *"The three fat women of Antibes"* came to life. He was joined by other English-language writers, including Julien Green and Anthony Burgess. Tragic events also played a part in creating this confluence: in 1943, Henry de Montherlant created a theatrical troupe for "Malesta" in Grasse, and Hans Hartung left the Foreign Legion for Antibes shortly thereafter. Before World War I, Thomas Mann had already talked of a "coast populated by madmen". Did he know that, for his *J'accuse*, Abel Gance had raised his dead of Verdun from the drained

[1] *American-born writer Julien Green, at the inauguration of an exhibition at the Picasso museum in Antibes, with the painter Paul Jenkins at the back.*

[2] *Belgian writer Maurice Maeterlinck (Ghent 1862 - Nice 1949) and his wife in* Palais Orlamonde *in Nice in August 1932.*

[3] *Author Jean-Marie G. Le Clézio was born in Nice before setting off for Africa and travelling all over the world to return to his birthplace.*

[4] *British writer William Somerset Maugham (Paris 1874 - Saint-Jean-Cap-Ferrat 1965) on the steps of the* Villa Mauresque *in Saint-Jean-Cap-Ferrat in 1948.*

trench-beds of the Var and Paillon rivers? During the next war, some of the finest masterpieces of cinema *(Les visiteurs du soir, Les enfants du paradis, L'éternel retour, Lumière d'été)* were shot in La Victorine studios in Nice, in a second heyday after the days of Rex Ingram in the 1920s. Alfred Hitchcock, Frankenheimer, Verneuil, Truffaut, Besson all chose to film here. The gold dust deposited on these works was inhaled by so many artists it would be impossible to name them all and continues to be dispersed all over the world.

SETTLEMENT AND ARCHITECTURE: work and reverie in stone

Weary travellers who finally put down their bags think they have reached the end of their journey. But do they know where they actually are? a Baroque Florida, a Rococo Piedmont, a Moorish Provence, a Belle-Époque Scotland, a mediaeval Ukraine, a Romanesque Paris? And the list could go on forever, with the almost haphazard blending and crossing of architectural styles, volumes and colours. They were first and foremost dictated by the needs of the time; though visual satisfaction, religious sentiment and a sense of nobility also had their part. And later, there was the grandiose elegance and delirious ostentation of residents who called upon a myriad of architects anxious to satisfy their every whim. To seek

1 *A* borie *in Caussols.*
These dry-stone corbelled
structures shaped like an
igloo with a domed roof and
a single, rather low entrance
(1.50 m) were built by
shepherds from the
17th to the 19th centuries.

2 *An example of*
20th-century architecture
by the AIA-CERA architectural
firm in the late 1980s.
It is in L'Arénas, the new
Business District of Nice
inaugurated in March 1989.

3 *First erected in 7 BC,*
the Emperor Augustus'
Trophy became a castle
in the Middle Ages and was
torn down in 1706.
It was not until 1901 that
the archaeologist Formigé
began excavating the Trophy
of the Alps. Later his son,
with the help of the
American Edward Tuck
from 1929 to 1933,
continued restoring the
monument. The limestone of
La Turbie used to build the
monument was quarried
nearby.

1 *The Mont-Alban Fort, to the East of Nice overlooking the Bay of Villefranche, was built in the 16th century.*

2 *The late 15th-century castle of Mouans-Sartoux was rebuilt in the 19th-century. Since 1990, it has housed a contemporary art centre,* Espace de l'Art Concret, *which organises exhibitions as well as concerts in the gardens.*

3 *The castle of Gourdon was rebuilt in 1610 on the foundations of a mediaeval fortress. It displays the trapezoid layout of many Provençal castles. Recently restored, it now houses a museum, with a fine collection of Naive Art.*

4 *In the 1920s and early 1930s, the houses in the area of Nice were decorated with plaster bas-reliefs and brightly coloured mosaics, which replaced the friezes on their façades.*

1. *Schist roofs in Saorge: ranging in size from 0.40 to 1 metre, the stone slabs or lauzes are irregular in shape.*

2. *The barns in the Tinée valley were built at altitudes of 800 to 2,000 m above sea level along trails used by transhumant herds and their shepherds.*

3. *Traditional house with souléaire: South-facing open attics that served for drying fruit, vegetables and cereals, all very important to the subsistence farming that characterised these inland regions.*

shelter from the heat and wind and contend with the rugged landscape, the local inhabitants had, for centuries, built their tall narrow village houses where "the donkey was stabled up on the third floor" and fruit were set out to dry on the top level. The resources available were few and the architectural forms were kept very simple, though livened up by yellow, ochre or red rendering, trompe-l'œil decoration, paintings and friezes, lintels and sundials, woodwork painted pale or dark green, brown, rust or blue. For those fearing monotony, there is always the charm of a Baroque or Romanesque detail on a sacred structure, the martial note on an arcaded square or the crystalline sound of a fountain around a corner. Whether inspired

by the Provençal or Ligurian styles or simply that of the mountains, the *bastides*, barns and sheepfolds blend the use of limestone, red terra cotta tiles, schist, larchwood or rye-thatch roofing. But, to accommodate grandiose explosions of light, conceal more or less illicit loves, reconstruct faraway worlds even with their flora, more impressive stone naves were erected. On the

1 A Belle-Epoque palace in Menton : today, some of these fine homes on the heights of Menton have been converted into medical institutions subsidised by the General Council of the Alpes-Maritimes département.

2 The former 18th-century palace of Count Saïsi de Châteauneuf in Blausasc was recently restored by the current owner.

3 *A villa amid palm trees in Menton. The railway reached Menton in 1896, thereby contributing to the onslaught of winter visitors who built splendid homes and made the city into a very popular winter resort with over 50 hotels and 250 villas.*

4 *Many of the fine villas on the Cap-Martin were built between 1889 and 1910 by the Danish architect Hans Georg Tiersling in a Neo-classical or sometimes Renaissance style.*

hills and the seafront, immense hotels raised their façades like vertical parks to "separate the rest of the world from the great of this world" feasting in their staterooms. Although they now have a more staid vocation, the *Orient Palace* in Menton, the *Excelsior Regina Palace* or the *Grand Palais* in Nice still echo with these past fêtes. In the parks of Neo-classical or

1

2

Aristocratic visitors, who travelled with their families and a large staff of servants, were accommodated in some fifty large hotels. In addition to the splendid environment, they demanded the level of luxury and comfort they had become accustomed to in the European capitals.

1 *The* Excelsior Régina Palace *in Nice is the crowning glory of an ambitious urban project sponsored by a banker and a perfumer in 1895 and designed by the famous architect S.M. Biasini of Nice in 1897-1898.*

2 *The Carlton in Cannes, built in 1911, offers 355 rooms and suites.*

3 *The* Grand Hôtel du Cap-Ferrat, *surrounded by terraced gardens down to the sea, was designed by Martinet in 1908.*

4 *The* Palais California *in Cannes was built in 1876 by the architect Vianez in typical Neo-classical style.*

5 *The Hôtel Vistaero on the Grande Corniche. Built on the site of a wooden relay station of 1870, this luxury hotel with its panoramic view was last rebuilt in 1987 by a local architect on the initiative of a German firm.*

gingerbread châteaux, the statues of Fabron, Valrose, La Californie or La Croix des Gardes display the melancholy or eccentricities of hosts as colourful as they were mad and their impressive staff of servants. The hosts have gone, but there remain the trees with such exotic names as araucaria, dracæna or chamerops. Women have been a source of inspiration for some of the finest villas: Eilen Roc at Cap d'Antibes, Fiesole in Cannes, Villa Ephrussi de Rothschild in Saint-Jean-Cap-Ferrat. "Never will we have seen so many centuries and latitudes combined in such a small space," exclaimed a 19th-century witness who would miss out on the next century's many novelties: after the whipped cream buildings topped with garlands, fruit, masks and

*A*ntti Lovag's anti-architecture. Great eyes gobble up light as the rounded protuberances of multiple orifices evoke some strange sort of coupling or ingestion. Could it be a sea monster straight out of the abyssal depths, grounded on the rocks and seeking refuge among the vegetation? No, this apparent red-skinned cephalopod is not a living organism. It is lived in, however, and is the work of a "habitologist". This is how Antti Lovag defines himself. A trained architect, he has broken with his profession and the standardised rules of urban planning. He is less concerned with the outer shell than with how the occupants cope with energy, experience their privacy, take possession of their dwelling space and incorporate it in the environment, were it one day through self-construction. The result most often is curvaceous volumes, sensuous in nature and indestructible in structure. From Théoule overlooking the sea all the way to the lunar Plateau de Calern, Antti Lovag has installed his hollow stones. A vital lead to be followed by those who do not despair of the architectural future in the land of bories.

1 *HLM La Minière (public housing) in an old factory in Saint-Dalmas-de-Tende (1978 - architect Thierry Valfort) was one of the first examples of the rehabilitation of abandoned industrial buildings put to a completely new use.*

2 Fondation du Futur, *founded by the writer Martin Gray in the Tanneron mountains, was designed by Thierry Valfort in 1990 around a black granite pond. It was built to host meetings of artists, scientists, writers and young people from all horizons.*

3 *The new Mediterranean architecture: Villa B. Cardi at Col de Villefranche, designed by the architect Guy Rottier who worked with Le Corbusier, then with Jean Prouvé in the 1950s.*

4 *Charles Barberis's villa in Villeneuve Loubet, built in 1962 by Guy Rottier.*

5 *"La Coupole" cultural centre built in 1988 by the architect D. Petry-Amiel, who calls it: "a recreational structure in response to the cultural aspirations of [the village of] La Gaude". It houses Ib Schmedes's collection of live insects.*

6 *La Chambre d'Agriculture des Alpes-Maritimes in La Gaude was built by D. Petry-Amiel to be "a citadel in which to debate the value of agriculture, the last protected bastion in a département with a vocation for tourism."*

other ornaments, glazed tiles, wrought-iron balconies
and glass to light up even the stairwells and lifts, there
followed the Art Deco style. From these books written
in stone and which can be perused through the streets,
along the roads, there are some missing pages, torn
out by the vicissitudes of time and some builders' hasty
appetite. Others have been scratched out negligently to
be excused. Life is so wonderful, everyone wants to
enjoy it. The latest forms - and the first ones visitors see
- are the geometric lines along the main cities' seafront
marked by broad balconies with picture windows and
multicoloured awnings, sometimes reflected in the
smoked glass façades of office buildings. In the sublime
as in the immoral, nothing here is ever commonplace.

1 *L'Arenas district arose
from an economic and
architectural wager.
This project by major
architects of Nice was
to propose in the 1980s a
consistent coherent complex
with parvis, office buildings,
hotels and parks, on 14 ha
of grounds, 130,000 m²
of structures adjacent
to* Parc Floral Phœnix.

2 *Martin Gray's* Fondation
du Futur *in the Tanneron
mountains (1990 - architect
Thierry Valfort) is arranged
like an amphitheatre built
with tank caterpillars,
a fountain created from
scraps of marble.*

3 *Asian Arts Museum:
according to the architect
Kenzo Tange, "our main
concept was to imagine a
very light structure floating
like a swan on the lake...
The layout is based on
the square, symbolising
the earth, and the circle,
symbolising the sky."
Kenzo Tange is a key figure
in Japanese architecture.*

4 *Aerial view of Marina
Baie des Anges and its
harbour. Shaped like a wave
around a little yachting
harbour, the four sections
were built by the Minangoy
architectural firm starting
in 1968 for* L'Amiral, *while*
Le Commodore *was
completed in 1972,*
Le Baronnet *in 1989 and*
Le Ducal *in 1992.*

1 *The history of the bread oven goes far back in time. Villagers took turns heating the community oven to bake bread, tarts and pies and fougasses.*

2 *Wheat, rye and barley were staples for the inhabitants of the hinterland, as attested by these village houses topped by attics facing South to lay out crops to dry.*

3 *Grapes have been grown since the Middle Ages in Villars, whose wine enjoys the AOC Côtes-de-Provence appellation. The vineyard of Bellet in Nice is one of the oldest in France, founded in ancient Phocaean times.*

4 *The olive tree personifies Provence, both the emblem of its culture and its art of living. It was imported from Asia by Phocaean Greeks in the 6th century BC. The olive tree can live several centuries and always remains productive. Its fruit was long the main resource for a large number of villages located at altitudes under 700 metres above sea level. They inspired the Impressionist painter Auguste Renoir to say: "Look at the light on the olive trees, shining like a diamond. It is pink, it is blue and the sky playing through the foliage is enough to drive you mad!"*

CUISINE: a delight for the eyes and the palate

Ah cruel celebrity! The cuisine of Nice has been round the world, though sometimes under a false identity. "I've been served other people's leftovers under the name *Salade Niçoise*," complained Jacques Médecin indignantly. As Mayor of Nice, he often wrote to vaunt the virtues of a culinary tradition that is too often unjustly debased, even in its homeland, or relegated to a Provençalo-Mediterranean hotchpotch reduced to the most basic ingredients: oil, olives, garlic and rosé wine. Take the olive "very delicately," warned the poet Mistral. The fruit of the *cailletier,* the tiny blackish pebble bears little resemblance to its brethren from elsewhere in Provence: Les Baux or even the Var département. As in the past, "traditionalists"can still take their olives to an oil mill and, at the end

1 *Between Menton and Antibes, from February 1 to April 30, the fishermen pull in the "beach seines" bringing in tiny fish for frying and* poutina. *This fishing technique involves scraping the grassy seafloor with a net (the seine) to catch sardine fry, or alevins, known as* "poutina", *eaten fried, in fritters or in an omelette.*

2 *The local fish include sardines, anchovies,* bugues, *red mullet, sea bream, scorpionfish, rainbow wrasse, dory ; they all have their place among the ingredients of* bouillabaisse, *the fish stew famous throughout the region.*

of the day, partake of *"brissauda"*, a broad slice of grilled bread rubbed with garlic and drenched in virgin olive oil. Rustic and fragrant, the "dessert of the mill" is in the very image of the cuisine of the old Comté de Nice. It is in a way the counterpart of the *"merenda"*, almost an early morning snack, if the word were not excessive for "a tomato with a salted anchovy fillet and a dribble of olive oil". This "land of plenty", as Vauban qualified it after seeing a fig tree, an olive tree and vine all growing on the same *restanque* (narrow agricultural terrace), would have been gratified had the military engineer's description actually reflected the truth. But with very little *charcuterie* (delicatessen meats) and just a little bit more fish caught in the *"cales"* (inlets) of Villefranche, Carras, and especially

Cros-de-Cagnes by fishermen in their *"pointus"* (barques), all these resources were carefully worked out : *"poutina"* and red mullet fished off the rocks become something unforgettable. From the harsh steep slopes, women over the centuries have done their best in the consummate art of transforming chick-pea flour into "chips" à la Niçoise *("panisses")* or a sunburst of *"socca"* and using the omnipresent chard in ravioli or tarts and pies, savoury and sweet, flavoured with brandy and orange-blossom water. To accompany *daube* (beef stewed in wine), ratatouille or *estocaficada* (stockfish) with its persistent "fierce stench", there used to be quite a selection; vine was grown on the slopes of Valdeblore, or along the Roya and Vésubie rivers. The vineyards have survived in Saint-Roman-de-Bellet on land worth

3 *Local culinary specialities include chard pie, Salade Niçoise, socca, tiny stuffed vegetables, and of course pissaladière, baked along with the bread, to test the heat of the oven. It was made with bread dough, rolled out to form a tart filled with onion fried in olive oil with anchovies cured in salt* (peis sala), *hence the name,* peis-sala diero, *which became pissaladière.*

4 *Bouillabaisse being prepared with fish, fennel, aïoli (garlic mayonnaise), croutons and tomatoes.*

A city wine: ever since it was discovered by Catinat, Field Marshal for French King Louis XIV, although it did not preserve the Citadel of Nice from his destructive wrath, the wine of Bellet has restored in the hearts of œnologists (wine connoisseurs) the celebrity it had acquired in Antiquity. But its reputation is far greater than the size of its vineyards. They are no bigger on the map than Carnival confetti: under fifty hectares of slopes of sand and pebbles, facing West, where many city-dwellers would love to relax, were it not for a handful of indomitable aficionados of such varieties of vine as Braquet, Folle noire, Cinsault, Rolle, Spagnol or Roussan. Whether from a long line of vine growers or fresh converts, they are huddled around the Château de Crémat and their production of 300,000 bottles barely suffice to delight the finest tables with their lovely ruby reds, rosés recalling the fragrance of "iris root" and whites that are so amazingly fresh in such a sun-drenched land.

[1] Antoine Mari, a wealthy owner of olive groves, built the Château de Crémat on the ridge of the hill of Crémat in the early 20th century on the remains of a Roman watchtower. He created a pilot vineyard, privileging local varieties. He set up transatlantic freight and introduced his wine to US bluebloods. Under his château, the immense cellars, excavated by the ancient Romans, are made up essentially of two vaulted galleries each 50 metres long and 4 to 10 metres deep. Today, the château has been completely restored by the new owner, Jean-Pierre Pisoni, giving the Château de Crémat vineyards a new lease on life.

[2] The Château de Bellet de Charnacé was built in the typical tradition of Nice, its ochre façades decorated with trompe-l'œil painting and two round towers. This wine-growing estate has been held by the same family for four centuries. Ghislain de Charnacé shares his passion for wine with a handful of wine-growers from the hills who defend this precious heritage on the heights of Crémat, Saquier and Saint-Roman.

[1] In this region, each hive can hold 50,000 worker bees and produce 15 kg of honey a year. The honey differs according to the location of the hives. One of the finest is honey made from lavender, but there is also delectable honey from rosemary, mixed flowers or pine forest. The honey is harvested once a season, by filling the hive with smoke.

[2] Harvesting linden flowers for a popular herbal tea.

[3] The persimmon tree is from Asia. In the hills of Nice, its suave fruit stand out like Chinese lanterns as they ripen into a bright orange colour in autumn when the leaves have fallen off the tree.

[4] Wild boletus mushrooms, or cèpes, grow in the chestnut and oak forests of the hinterland. Today, their harvest is strictly regulated.

[5] Truffles: tuber melanosporum is a dark brown fungus buried deep under the feet of various deciduous trees, especially oak, in sunny locations on limestone. They grow in winter in the hinterland of Nice and Grasse, where dogs are used to find and unearth them .

Page 225: Agricultural activities in the region include growing fruit, picking wild mushrooms, making bread, cheese and wine.

its weight in gold, making Nice the only city to produce *"AOC"* wine, and, more modestly, in Villars-sur-Var. But they have been revived on the Isle of Saint-Honorat and south of the *"Baccus"* (instead of *"baous"*), to quote a most fortunate misprint in a tourist brochure. These estates, no larger than gardens, are sometimes tended by monks, artists or art dealers. Art is never very far away from gastronomy. On the great tables scattered over the land, like a star-studded "Milky Way" in all the guidebooks, courgettes, local artichokes, asparagus, young fava beans and basil or mint leaves picked early in the morning in Lingostière, Auribeau or Gattières, when presented on a plate become a perpetual feast for the eyes and for the palate.

Specialities of Nice and Provence made with olive oil: pistou *with sweet basil and garlic,* tapenade *with black olives, anchovies, capers and thyme,* anchoïade *with anchovies and olive oil, bell peppers with olive oil and garlic, stuffed courgette blossoms,* tian *of courgettes, red squash or* cougourdons, *the* pan-bagnat *made with a round loaf of bread soaked in olive oil with tomatoes, bell peppers, scallions, anchovies, hard-boiled eggs, tiny black olives and garlic.*

*O*live oil. Oil with fennel, pimento, rosemary, thyme, bay leaf, marjoram, garlic, etc. And to find what to eat it with, there are limitless possibilities, only Nature and imagination can set the bounds. Neither is lacking in the largest - and best tended - olive grove in France. There are no uniform alignments as in Andalusia. Trimmed like lace on their bed of daisies awaiting the winter fruit, the tree of Pallas Athena is the object of considerable attention, and rightfully so. Of all the plants grown here, more than any other it deserves its image as the truly emblematic species of the entire Provençal region. In the famous accounts of his travels in the early 19th century, François Fodéré ecstatically admired the fact that it "grows as easily as the fir trees in the upper Alps; it reaches a size and height equal to the finest walnut trees." The little black olives, nibbled along with anisette or ground in the ancestral tradition by the millstone of the 25 oil mills, are grown and picked by more than 6,000 people, for 1,620 of whom it is their livelihood, on some 4,000 hectares of land and supplying 500 metric tons of olives and 400 metric tons of oil. Now, is there any exaggeration in the assertion that the olive of Nice is the fruitiest and its oil the most fragrant in the Mediterranean? No, just take the time to taste them.

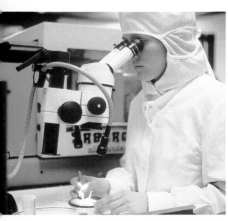

FUTURE PROSPECTS:
the most favourable auspices

The third millennium will open up new horizons for global tourism. This is good news for the Alpes-Maritimes, second only after Paris on the list of favourite destinations: 8 million visitors come here each year, making this venue as popular as Greece or the Caribbean. The Alpes-Maritimes has a key role to play in the organisation of Mediterranean tourism. All visitors coming here have over a thousand hotels and residences at their fingertips, the highest concentration of world-class luxury establishments, an extraordinary range of 30,000 rooms, up to ten casinos, an incomparable number of restaurants and a variety of bistros and entertainment opportunities. All these sectors provide a major source of livelihood for the

Grey matter has taken over from raw materials. Shortly after Cannes greeted the first starlets on its beaches, such companies as IBM, Texas Instruments and Thomson CSF pioneered the way to these peaceful rural surroundings, lighting the digital revolution alongside the already powerful aromatics industry. Born ten years later from an even more daring challenge, Sophia Antipolis represents the outcome of the dynamic creativity that propelled the Alpes-Maritimes into a world of infinite speed (networks, software engineering, space) and infinitesimal life forms (pharmaceuticals, biotechnology).

1 *SkyBridge: a constellation of 80 satellites for interactive multimedia services (Alcatel Space Industries in Cannes)*

2 *From the Plateau de Calern overlooking the village of Caussols (1,200 m above sea level), astronomers have calculated the precise distance between the Earth and the moon thanks to the laser beam shown here.*

population. But the future also promises change. The winter tourism of crowned heads and courtesans gave way to the summer tourism first of dandies, then of sun worshippers. The distinction between high season and off-season gradually dimmed. Time never stops as luxury yachts cruise past this seafront, one of their favourite haunts. The palm trees facing the sea are no longer surprised by the swimsuit-clad tourists or the briefcase-wielding businessmen seeking respite in their shade. They may even be one and the same and such confusion of genres is no coincidence. When it was first created, after World War II, the Cannes Film Festival was no more than a stage for a beach resort. "The weather is splendid... much better than the films," muttered the poet Paul Éluard. Now, though, attending the "FIF" (to use the journalistic acronym) has become a must for anyone involved in motion pictures. It has attracted many other prestigious events associated with the world of communication, including television, music and multimedia. Standing amid some half-dozen towns, the "European Boulevard of Convention Centres" offers tens of thousands of square metres of exhibition space, 120 meeting rooms, nearly 300 hotels fully equipped for seminars and a myriad of service providers (translation, production, sound, etc.). One million participants flock here for the launch of the latest models of automobiles, or to discover the latest advances in medical science. This is where businesspersons and stars come together, from their homes in Peymeinade, Le Rouret or Cap-Martin, or simply stepping off their magnificent yachts. Some have ties with the local economy through

[1] *In 1998, approximately 8 million passengers went through the Riviera International Airport, with direct connections worldwide. The south runway was entirely built on the sea.*

[2] *Freight transport in a cargo plane on a runway at the Riviera International Airport.*

[3] *Terminal 1 at the Riviera International Airport and its recent extension for arrivals (Architects: Charles Jean Schmelz and Michel Orselli).*

[4] *Virtual view of the future terminal at the Riviera International Airport (Architects: Aéroports de Paris, Paul Andreu).*

The greening of grey matter. "Alive, envied and imitated," but never matched. More than thirty years after its birth, like a sort of futuristic mushroom in the midst of a rabbit warren occupying an immense pine grove, Sophia Antipolis has become the very symbol of the now widespread concept of the Technopole, or Science and Technology Park. It is a crucible where neuronal energy, creative ambition and art come together to create an admirable alloy, a cauldron blending them all in cross-fertilisation. This image was devised by Senator Pierre Laffitte, the Park's founder, who sought to bring ancient Attica and Renaissance Tuscany to Provence in the 21st century. As Director of L'Ecole des Mines, he first inspired the notion of a "City of wisdom, science and technology", in which the first building was a theatre, and made it convincing. It grew into an economic and social reality, made up of thousands of executives, technicians, engineers and researchers from 50 different countries. They work within several hundred businesses, laboratories, educational institutions (engineering schools). These establishments are famous worldwide in the fields of information technology and the life sciences in an architectural setting that fully respects the surrounding landscape. "A campus in the country", so unlike most French universities, Sophia Antipolis wishes to remain a source of amazement.

1 2 3 4 *World tourism will rise anew in the third millennium. This is an exciting prospect for the Alpes-Maritimes. Second most popular destination in France after Paris, the region welcomes powerful industrialists and media stars with homes in Peymeinade, Le Rouret or Cap-Martin, some just stepping out of their Rolls Royces or off luxury yachts.*

5 6 *Second-generation Météosat and Eutelsat W2 satellite (Alcatel Space Industries in Cannes).*

At the Oceanological Observatory in Villefranche (P. & M. Curie/Paris VI University and the CNRS), the Zoology Station has been studying deep-sea fauna (plankton) for over a century.

7 *Samples are still caught with conventional plankton nets, but mostly with multiple Bioness closing nets triggered by various computer programs and equipped with sensors for analysing the water's physicochemical parameters in real time.*

8 *This device is for taking video shots of floating organisms. After processing, they provide particle counts and measurements and identification of the living organisms encountered as the apparatus is submerged.*

subsidiarie or research centres. Many of these pan-European companies and management centres benefit from outside capital. Economic globalisation is nothing new. In the wake of the aromatics, the first to find their way into foreign trade, flowers were shipped by the trainload in the early 20th century to bring their sublime fragrance to northern climes. In addition to horticulture, olives, pottery and glassware are all ambassadors for the region. But now grey matter has taken over from raw materials. Shortly after Cannes greeted the first starlets on its beaches, such companies as IBM, Texas Instruments and Thomson CSF pioneered the way to these peaceful rural surroundings, lighting the digital revolution alongside the already powerful aromatics industry. Born ten years after an even more daring challenge, Sophia Antipolis represents the outcome of the dynamic creativity that propelled the Alpes-Maritimes into a world of infinite speed (networks, software engineering, space) and infinitesimal life forms (pharmaceuticals, biotechnology). The Park, the size of the historic core of Paris, lies at the centre of a fabric of activity areas teeming with productive SMEs connected to the entire world through a state-of-the-art telecommunications network and the second largest international airport in France. Located on the Mediterranean Arc linking Barcelona with the main industrial centres in northern Italy, with a strong southward orientation, the Alpes-Maritimes offers tremendous assets for the future development of Europe... on condition it loses none of the charms that have always made it so attractive.

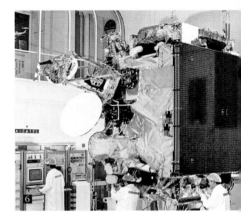

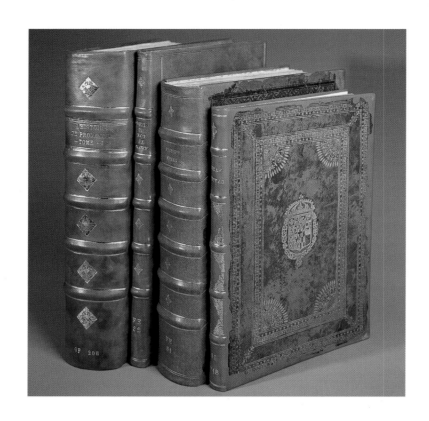

LAND OF HISTORY

From the Lower Palaeolithic strata in the Vallonnet Cave to the protohistoric Castellaras, the many archaeological remains in the Alpes-Maritimes retrace evolution from the first humans to the foundation of Antibes and Nice by the Greeks and the creation of the Roman *Alpes Maritimae* province. In the Middle Ages, Nice and its vicinity formed the eastern march of Provence, from which it separated to seek the protection of the Count of Savoy (1388). This reinforced the region's strategic and military role since it became Savoy's only access to the sea. In the brilliant heyday of Baroque art, the Savoyard rulers invested in the development of the Comté de Nice, instituting a free port in Nice in 1612, starting excavation of Port Lympia in 1748, upgrading the road from Nice to Cuneo over the Col de Tende after 1780. In the 18th century, foreigners, most of them from Britain, began flocking to Nice and paved the way for the tourism that would make the French Riviera so prosperous. Then, the French Revolution and Empire brought these developments to a halt. The Var département included the *arrondisssements* of Grasse and Saint-Paul. On September 29, 1792, French troops entered Nice and soon the entire Comté, plus the Principality of Monaco, was annexed to France to form the Alpes-Maritimes département. With the fall of the First Napoleonic Empire, the King of Sardinia recovered his former States. But he also acquired the former Republic of Genoa, so the province of Nice ceased to be his only outlet onto the sea. Yet, on each side of the border formed by the Var River, foreign visitors returned to the land of sunshine, like Lord Brougham in Cannes and tourism prospered as never before. In 1860, by the Treaty of March 24, freely concluded and approved by a virtually unanimous vote of the population, the *circondario* of Nice became French as the Alpes-Maritimes département to which were added the *arrondissement* of Grasse and the free towns of Menton and Roquebrune. Finally the peace treaty of February 10, 1947, reintegrated the communes of Tende and La Brigue. Today, the département has become world-famous, thanks to this remarkable era of expansion.

Detail of the mural (Museum of Terra Amata).

The Alpes-Maritimes is particularly rich in prehistoric sites, representing all the major stages in human evolution since Man first set foot on European soil. The primitive pebble tools found in the Vallonnet Cave date back one million years; 400,000 years ago at Terra Amata, Man had learned to tame fire; 100,000 years ago, Man occupied many caves, like Lazaret and Grimaldi, where the first signs of art were discovered.

THE FIRST HUMANS

One million years ago. The Vallonnet Cave in Roquebrune-Cap-Martin is one of the oldest known well-dated prehistoric sites in Europe. Some 950,000 to 900,000 years ago, hunters used very archaic tools to cut up the carcasses of animals: chipped pebbles and bones and flake tools. They did not have fire and the organisation of this occupation site was very rudimentary, but shows they lived in groups.

400,000 YEARS AGO

Man discovered how to control fire. Some 400,000 years ago, someone left a right footprint on the site of Terra Amata in Nice, where one of the oldest known hearths was discovered. On the slopes of Mont-Boron, a tiny inlet, then on the seashore, attracted bands of hunters who set up camp for brief seasonal occupations in late spring or early summer.

They built a hut on the beach, with branches supported by posts driven into the ground and a hearth at the centre, either on pebbles used to pave the ground, or in a shallow pit dug into the sand. To protect the flames from draughts especially from the north-west, they raised a low wall of stones or pebbles. Inside the huts, some areas were used for chipping tools and animal bones,

Pachyderm bone used as a tool (photograph: City of Nice, Museum of Terra Amata)

Chopper from Vallonnet Cave, one of the oldest tools found in Europe (photograph: City of Nice, Museum of Terra Amata)

while the floor was strewn with the remains of meals, making it possible to reconstruct the fauna pursued by these ancient hunters: elephant, wild boar, deer, cattle and rabbit.

200,000 YEARS AGO

On the slopes of Mont-Boron less than 100 metres from the present shores of the Mediterranean, the Lazaret Cave has delivered secrets of daily life some 130,000 years ago. To protect themselves from the cold in winter, they sought refuge in the cave, where they built a hut, 11 metres long to accommodate about ten people, against one of the walls of the cave and supported by posts. It was probably covered with animal skins. A low wall, 50 centimetres high, protected it from the wind from the sea penetrating through the entrance to the cave. Inside the hut, there were two hearths directly on the ground. These prehistoric hunters' favourite game included deer, ibex, horse, cattle, rhinoceros, elephant and especially rabbit. They also hunted wolf, fox, marmot, lynx and panther for their fur, the skins were thrown onto beds of marine algae, to make them more comfortable. The cranial bone of a 9-year-old child who died of meningioma (a meningeal tumour) was discovered in the Lazaret Cave, one of

Homo sapiens discovered art, decorating their caves with paintings and carvings of the animals around them (the horse of Grotte du Cavillon). And they wore jewellery: necklaces and ornaments made of shell and animal teeth. The skeletons found in Grotte des Enfants provide a fine example of burial rites in the Upper Palaeolithic.

The entrance to the Lazaret Cave in Nice (photograph: City of Nice, Museum of Terra Amata, A. Malaval).

the oldest human skull remains found to date in Europe.

50,000 YEARS AGO

Neanderthal Man showed the first signs of spiritual concerns and the desire to know something about the afterlife. They buried their dead with various offerings for this mysterious journey.

Neanderthals lived in true villages made up of huts covering a few square metres each, and in caves or rock shelters. They were excellent hunters whose collective techniques enabled them to attack animals as fierce as bears or panthers. During hunting expeditions, they sought shelter in caves on steep slopes, like Pié Lombard Cave in Tourrettes-sur-Loup, where a Neanderthal tooth was found.

20,000 YEARS AGO

The Grimaldi Caves on the Italian border were first occupied between 280,000 and 120,000 years ago (*Grotte du Prince*), but most of the archaeological remains date back 35,000 to 10,000 years. *Homo sapiens* discovered art, decorating their caves with paintings and carvings of the animals around them (the horse of *Grotte du Cavillon*). And they wore jewellery: necklaces and ornaments made of shell and animal teeth.

Grimaldi Caves: the burial in Grotte des Enfants (photograph: City of Nice, Museum of Terra Amata, A. Malaval).

Grimaldi Caves: Aurignacian Venus figurines, discovered in Barma Grande (photograph: City of Nice, Museum of Terra Amata, A. Malaval).

The skeletons found in the *Grotte des Enfants* provide a fine example of burial rites in the Upper Palaeolithic.

Vallée des Merveilles: the sorcerer.

IN NEOLITHIC TIMES, MAN PRACTISED FARMING AND HERDING, AND DEVELOPED THE TECHNIQUE OF MAKING POLISHED STONE TOOLS, DISCOVERED POTTERY-MAKING AND THE USE OF COPPER. THE PETROGLYPHS IN VALLÉE DES MERVEILLES DATE FROM THE CHALCOLITHIC (COPPER AGE) AND EARLY BRONZE AGE. IN THE IRON AGE, THE LIGURIANS BUILT MANY FORTIFIED SITES OR CASTELLARAS.

HERDSMEN IN VALLÉE DES MERVEILLES AND LIGURIAN FARMERS

During the Neolithic, 6,000 years BC, humans abandoned their predatory nomadic life to become sedentary and produce their own food. They became farmers and herdsmen and built the first stone villages. They invented the art of pottery-making (*c.* 5,500 BC), and made new polished stone artefacts (axes, adzes) and learned how to use copper in the late Neolithic. From the end of the Neolithic to the Bronze Age, we have megalithic monuments, dolmens and menhirs, like the *tumulus de Sainte-Anne* near Saint-Vallier and the *dolmen de Peyraoutes* near Roquefort-les-Pins, huge stone tombs in which the dead were buried following funerary rites (cremation, offerings).

Around Mont-Bego, Vallée des Merveilles and Vallée de Fontanalba, shaped by the glaciers of the Quaternary Era, were covered with thousands of late Neolithic and early Bronze Age rock carvings (2800-1800 BC).

In this spectacular landscape, herdsmen from the nearby coast or the plain of the Piedmont, carved their concerns and myths in true symbolic language: horned shapes, yokes, tools and weapons, anthropomorphic figures, reticulates and various other shapes.

Vallée des Merveilles: the "Tribal chief" (photograph: City of Nice, Museum of Terra Amata, J. Auguin)

Neolithic pottery from La Baume Périgaud, Saint-André (photograph: City of Nice, Museum of Terra Amata, J. Auguin).

In the Iron Age, the local populations were called Ligurians by the writers of the ancient world. Conflicts broke out between Ligurian tribes and great "Cyclopean" dry-stone strongholds were built. These enclosures, called *oppida* or Castellaras, are particularly common in south-eastern France. More than 350 have been identified in the Alpes-Maritimes, in particular on the Mont-Chauve, Mont-Bastide near Èze and La Piastre near Lucéram.

Greek inscription on the Terpon pebble, 5th or 4th century BC (Archaeology museum of Antibes). "I am Terpon, servant of the august Aphrodite; may Cypris favour those who placed me here."

Antibes and Nice, two colonies founded by Phocaean Greeks from Marseille in the mid-6th century, were threatened in the 2nd century by the Ligurians. The Romans were called to help overcome the local populations, and in the reign of the Emperor Augustus the Alpine tribes were finally vanquished and the Alpes Maritimae province founded. A great road, Via Julia Augusta, then linked all the land from Italy to Spain.

THE GREEK COLONIES AND THE ROMAN CONQUEST 6TH - 1ST CENTURY BC

In the mid-6th century, the Phocaeans settled in Marseille set up new colonies on the coast, in Antibes (Antipolis) and Nice (Nikaia). Contacts were made between the Greek merchants and the Ligurian peoples, with exchanges of ceramics and silver against medicinal and aromatic plants and ore. But relations were not always peaceful and the Ligurians posed a threat to the two cities. In 154 BC, Marseille called Rome to the rescue of these colonies. The military campaigns of 123-121 BC led to the permanent presence of Romans in the broad region known as *Provincia*, from the Alps to the Pyrenees. A certain number of Alpine tribes remained independent, however, east of the Var River. In spite of Caesar's campaign in Gaul in 52 BC, the peoples of the Alps were still a threat and a source of insecurity for communication between the Italian peninsula, Southern Gaul and Spain. From 25 to 14 BC, the conquest of the Alps was completed by the Emperor Augustus, making it possible to build a land route along the coast: the *Via Aurelia* was prolonged in Gaul by the *Via Julia Augusta*. To celebrate this event and the victory it represented, in 6 BC, the Roman Senate had a huge Trophy of white marble erected on

Augustus' Trophy (7 BC): in 1901 the archaeologist Formigé began its restoration.

Wine amphora, 1st century BC (Archaeology museum of Antibes).

the pass marking the border between Gaul and Italy, at La Turbie. In this strategic region, the Romans instituted the *Alpes Maritimae* province with a military administration, headquartered in Cemenelum (Cimiez), the former *oppidum* of the Vediantii. On its hilltop, Nice remained dependent on Marseille until the early 3rd century AD, while Antibes freed itself in 43 BC to become a *municipium* in the Roman *Provincia*.

Thanks to the Pax Romana, the Alpes Maritimae province developed rapidly, as shown by the urbanisation of some sites, particularly in the 2nd century for Antibes and the 3rd century for Cimiez, capital of the province. The decadence of imperial Rome led to the decline of Cimiez, which lost its rank as capital of the Alpes Maritimae to the town of Embrun in the 4th century. Cimiez enjoyed a brief revival in the late 5th century as a bishop's see.

Dancing faun, bronze statuette 1ˢᵗ century AD, found in Cimiez (height: 26cm)

THE ALPES MARITIMAE PROVINCE
1ST - 5TH CENTURY

The *Alpes Maritimae* province enjoyed four centuries of *Pax Romana*. The sites occupied by Ligurians were gradually abandoned in favour of more hospitable places. Romanisation rapidly spread from the coast to the hinterland. The population grew wheat, olives and wine and raised sheep. Towns were built: the capital Cemenelum (Cimiez), Vintium (Vence), Brigantio or Brigomagus (Briançonnet) and Glanate (Glandèves) as well as Antibes, which was particularly prosperous in the 2nd century, with the lucrative trade in *garum*, a tuna-based condiment very popular with the Romans.

In the mid-3rd century, Cimiez, originally no more than a residence for the governor and the garrison, was more fully urbanised. This was the most brilliant period for the provincial capital, marked by the construction of the main monuments. Three bath complexes were built in the 2nd and 3rd centuries AD and the 1st-century arena was enlarged into an amphitheatre in the 3rd century. The town was never large, however, covering no more than 20 hectares, where a small population lived from crafts, transport and trade and loyally worshipped the Emperor. The 3rd century was also

Bracelets found on Mont-Gros

marked by evangelisation with the legendary martyrdom of Saint Bassus and Saint Pons and the miraculous arrival of Saint Reparata (253-258).

In 297, the province extended all the way to Embrun, which replaced Cimiez when the latter declined. After destruction in the late 4th century, Cimiez seems to have had a brief renascence with the establishment of a diocese in the 5th century. In the ruins of the western baths there is a Palaeo-Christian complex, with a basilica and baptistery surrounded by a few homes. But the bishopric of Cemenelum was attached to that of Nikaia by the end of the 5th century and the people sought refuge in the fortified hilltop *castellum* of Nikaia. In the 6th century the site of the ancient Roman town was completely abandoned.

Reliquary of Saint-Honorat, polychrome wood
(photograph: Graniou)

The 5th century in Western Europe was characterised by the Great Invasions. First held by the Visigoths, then the Ostrogoths, the land came under the domination of the Franks in the 6th century. Starting in the 9th century, the Saracens created a constant climate of insecurity until William, Count of Arles, expelled them at the end of the 10th century.

THE RISE OF CHRISTIANITY
5TH - 11TH CENTURY

In 412, the Visigoths, originally from the lower Danube, sacked Rome and entered Gaul via the region of Nice to found the Kingdom of Toulouse. The region then enjoyed relative tranquillity, which enabled Christianity to develop. C. 410, two hermits, Honorat and Caprais, founded the monastery of Lérins, a focus of Christian culture, which produced several bishops and theologians. Provence went from Visigoth rule to Ostrogoth domination in the early 6th century. In 536, the Franks, taking advantage of the Ostrogoths' weakening power, obtained Provence, which was invaded by the Lombards via the Durance valley.

In the early 8th century the Saracens began plundering the coast, in particular the monastery of Lérins. The treaty of Verdun (843) settled Charlemagne's succession, attributing Provence to Lothair, along with Burgundy and Italy (Lotharingia). When Lothair died, Lotharingia was fragmented (855). From 933 to 1032, Provence became part of the Kingdom of Burgundy-Provence. After the sack of Nice in the 9th century, the Saracens settled in the Maures massif and conducted raids throughout the region. Their capture of the abbot of Cluny caused such outrage that a coalition was formed

Early 5th-century sarcophagus, Abbey of Lérins (photograph: Graniou)

under the leadership of William, Count of Arles, who routed them c. 975. William, dubbed the "Liberator" became the unchallenged ruler of Provence.

In the 11th century, the fragmentation of power gave rise to feudalism. The population was grouped in "perched", fortified localities for reasons of security. To the secular power was added the temporal power of the bishops and monastic orders. Lérins lost its spiritual influence, but it received many donations in the 11th century and, in the 12th century, drew up all its privileges and donations in an invaluable cartulary. For their defence, the monks turned their abbey into a fortress after 1088.

Transcription of the Deed of 824 in the cartulary of the Abbey of Lérins, 12th century (Archives départementales)

Confirmation of the liberties and franchise of the City of Nice,
1245 (Archives municipales)

Until the end of the 14th century, the history of the Alpes-Maritimes is one with that of Provence, ruled in the 12th century and the first half of the 13th by the Counts of Catalonia, then, after 1246, by the Dukes of Anjou, Kings of Naples and Sicily. The Counts reinforced their authority at the expense of the nobles and the communes, and the boundaries extended to the Roya valley (1258) and the Piedmont (1259).

EASTERN PROVENCE IN THE MIDDLE AGES
1112 - 1342

From 1112 to 1245, Provence was ruled by the Catalan Counts of Barcelona. They clashed with the spirit of autonomy of the main barons and unrest in the major cities. The Counts' authority was reinforced and exemplified by the reign of Ramon-Berenguer V (1205-1245) who, with the support of his seneschal Romée de Villeneuve, organised the State. He set his capital in Aix and divided the Countship into bailiwicks. The demographic and economic growth of the communities in the 12th century promoted the emergence of consular institutions as in Italy (Nice, Grasse, Drap, Peille, etc.). In the early 13th century, Ramon-Berenguer V pursued the work of his grandfather Alfonso I (1166-1196) by undertaking to control the consulates that resisted his authority and, as in Nice, were strongly influenced by Genoa, which had taken over the Rock of Monaco in 1215. He successively imposed his rule in Grasse (1227) and Nice (1229) where he suppressed the consulates and appointed a bailiff and a viguier respectively. He entrusted the government of these newly controlled territories to Romée de Villeneuve.

In 1246, Ramon-Berenguer V's daughter Beatrice, wife of Charles I Duke of Anjou

Seal of Charles II of Anjou,
1285-1309
(Archives municipales)

(1246-1280), brother of the King of France Louis IX (Saint Louis). Charles I acquired the Roya valley from the Counts of Ventimiglia (1258) and settled in the southern Piedmont (1259). When the Pope offered him the crown of Sicily, he set out to conquer an empire in the Mediterranean. He became King of Naples and Sicily, but lost Sicily in 1282. His son Charles II (1285-1309) kept southern Italy and the southern Piedmont and, aware of the military value of the Bay of Villefranche, signed the deed founding the city of Villefranche and granting franchises to the inhabitants on August 8, 1295. In the peaceful reign of Robert (1309-1343), the administration of the Countship was further refined with the creation of *vigueries* regrouping the bailiwicks. But a new force was already emerging when a Grimaldi became Lord of Beuil in 1315. From the 11th to the 13th century, the network of castles grew and Romanesque art flourished. In the 14th century, the cities surrounded themselves with ramparts.

Secret promise by Louis Grimaldi to transfer the Countship of Provence to the Count of Savoy, 1388 (Archives départementales)

The succession of Queen Joan (1343-1382), heiress to the Countship of Provence and the Kingdom of Naples, resulted in a long civil war, exacerbated by terrible ordeals, such as the Black Death in 1348, famine and the ravages of bands of mercenaries and pirates. Encouraged by the Grimaldis of Beuil, the people of Nice accepted the protection of Amedeus VII, Count of Savoy (1383-1391): the "Dedition" of Nice to Savoy was signed in 1388. The region of Nice became a possession of Savoy; this was the time when such fine late Gothic painters as Durandi, Miralhet, Canavesio and Baleison flourished.

THE SECESSION OF NICE
1343 - 1492

In the mid-14th century, the region, after a time of relative prosperity, went through a turbulent period: strongly affected in 1348 by the Black Death, one of the worst plague epidemics to hit the Western world, then shaken by the Great Schism between Rome and Avignon, the region was also profoundly destabilised by the problems of the succession of Queen Joan. Desirous of annexing Provence, the French Crown attempted to have the authority of Louis of Anjou, brother of French King Charles V, recognised. But the strong resistance in the eastern part of the region resulted in complete anarchy. The Count of Savoy, threatened by the French policy of expansion, adroitly took advantage of the situation by dealing with the Grimaldis of Beuil and succeeded in prevailing. The negotiations resulted in the "Dedition" of 1388, by which Nice and the Ubaye valley separated from Provence. The Count of Savoy delegated his powers to a "governor of the city of Nice and the land of Provence".

The 15th century was for the region of Nice a time in which confraternities flourished and the profound religious feeling was expressed by an artistic awakening. The intense creativity was expressed in panel

Saint Margaret, painting in Saint-Dalmas-le-Selvage, discovered in 1996 and attributed to Baleison (photograph: Graniou)

paintings, murals in churches and chapels and works of art.

In 1482, when the Countship of Provence was annexed to France, the Var River became a border between the Royal Domain and the territories of Savoy. From then on, Nice acquired a major strategic role for the Duke with respect to his powerful neighbour.

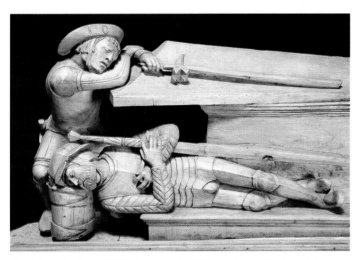

Sculpture in Puget-Théniers, early 16th century (photograph: Graniou)

Mont-Alban Fort in Nice (photograph: Graniou)

The artistic movement of the Renaissance is illustrated in the Comté de Nice by the Brea family, whose most famous representative, Ludovic, has left major works. Yet the 16th century was above all a century of unrest and war in the region, wars between France and Savoy and wars of Religion.

THE WARS OF THE RENAISSANCE
1493 - 1595

French King Francis I's Italian policy led him to claim his rights to Nice from the Duke of Savoy who was allied with the Emperor Charles V. The Holy Roman Emperor invaded Provence and the French entered the Piedmont in 1536, forcing Duke Charles III (1504-1553) to seek refuge in Nice with the Holy Shroud. The imperial troops pillaged the surroundings of Grasse. After a failed attempt at mediation by Pope Paul III between Francis I and Charles V, the Congress of Nice, in May 1538, the war resumed. In June 1543, the French army and their Turkish allies besieged Nice, which was plundered then abandoned as reinforcements arrived. Francis I's victory over Charles V enabled him to annex Savoy and part of the Piedmont, but he yielded the Comté de Nice. Thanks to the Treaty of Cateau Cambrésis in 1559, the new Duke Emmanuel Philibert (1553-1580) was able to recover most of his possessions, while France was caught up in the Wars of Religion. Drawing the lessons from the invasion of 1536, the Duke established his capital in Turin and reinforced his defences in the Comté during his stay in Nice in 1559-1560, building a bastioned fort on Mont-Alban and the Citadel of Villefranche. The Comté, Savoy's only outlet on the sea, acquired strategic importance that was essential for the Duke, while the acquisition of the Principality of Oneglia (1576) and the Countship of Tende (1579) facilitated his access from the Piedmont to the sea over the mountain passes. On the French side, tremendous efforts were made to reinforce the defences along the Provençal border by erecting the Fort Carré near Antibes and modernising the ramparts of Saint-Paul-de-Vence, which the French King had visited in 1538. Eastern Provence suffered considerably from the Wars of Religion, especially between 1590 and 1595, with *coups de main* and plundering, and the incursion of Savoyard troops come to the rescue of the Holy League. They captured Grasse, Vence and Antibes but when French King Henri IV abjured his Protestant faith and appointed the very Catholic Duc de Guise to be Governor of Provence this foreign occupation came to an end in 1595.

Castle of Cagnes: painted ceiling by Pietro Benso, representing the fall of Phaeton, early 17th century (photograph: Graniou)

The importance of Nice as the Savoyard States' only outlet on the Mediterranean Sea was materialised in the early 17th century by the creation of a free port and reinforcement of the institutions. This period of renewal of Catholicism witnessed the birth of Baroque art.

BAROQUE GRANDEUR
1596 - 1689

The 17th century was characterised by the reinforcement of the central power. In 1621 the Count of Beuil, Annibal Grimaldi, the last feudal lord to claim to escape the authority of the Duke of Savoy, was arrested and executed. The appointment of the first Intendant in 1688 reinforced the control of the power in Turin. For Nice, the 17th century was essentially a time of economic prosperity and expansion in spite of the last great plague epidemic to hit the region in 1631. The importance granted to Nice by the Duke is clear in the appearance of new institutions: the Senate founded in 1614, the Sea Consulate in 1616, the transformation of the school into a university in 1640. Most of all, after 1612, Nice benefited from its new status as a free port, for a boost to its trade. The renewal of Catholicism was expressed by the construction of many religious structures, in particular the new Sainte-Réparate cathedral (1650-1685). The triumph of Baroque art in Nice combines influences from the Piedmont and Liguria. Thus, the 17th century represents an essential moment in the artistic history of Nice through the importance of the Baroque, which marks its originality in relation to its Provençal roots. Baroque

Institution of the free port in Nice and Villefranche in 1612 (Archives départementales)

influence nonetheless extended across the Var River, as exemplified by the castle of Cagnes with its extraordinary painted ceiling by the Genoan fresco painter Benso. This period of the Counter-Reformation was characterised in Vence by the personality of the bishop Antoine Godeau, a major literary figure whose friendship with Cardinal Richelieu earned him entry into the newly founded *Académie Française*.

Entrance in Nice of Victor Amedeus II, Duke of Savoy. Oil on cavas, anonymous, between 1689 and 1713 (Fondation Humbert et Marie-José de Savoie Collection)

In the late 17th century Louis XIV undertook a policy of conquest that led him to occupy the Comté de Nice twice. Yet the diplomatic stakes and defeats left France only the viguerie of Barcelonnette on the southeastern border.

LOUIS XIV, THE SUN KING, COUNT OF NICE 1690 - 1715

In 1690, war resumed with Savoy - under French protectorate since 1630 - when Duke Victor Amedeus made an alliance with Spain. The fortress of Nice fell in 1691 and the occupation of Nice lasted five years but, in 1696, Louis XIV signed an unexpected peace treaty, returned Savoy and Nice and married his grandson to Victor Amedeus's daughter. Yet Louis XIV's ambitions led once again to a new European conflict when he accepted the Spanish succession in 1700. The alliance with Savoy was broken once more. War again brought French troops to Nice, which was captured in April 1705. Louis XIV then ordered the complete destruction of the Castle, which was razed to the ground in 1706, depriving Nice of its defensive capacity once and for all. The French army was defeated in Turin in 1706, with the result that Provence was invaded all the way to Toulon where the Savoyards failed before retreating. Nice was retaken by the French and occupied until the Treaty of Utrecht in 1713, which marked a turning point in the political history of the States of Savoy. The Comté de Nice lost the *Viguerie* of Barcelonnette, given to France, in exchange for Sicily, which granted the Duke of Savoy the title of King. The European

Description of the capture of Nice by Catinat, 1691 (Archives départementales)

diplomatic game forced Victor Amedeus, however, to give up Sicily to Spain in exchange for Sardinia in 1720. From then on, Savoy ruled the Sardinian States made up of four entities: Piedmont, Savoy, Nice and Sardinia.

Villa Furtado-Heine (1895) - originally built in 1787 by Lady Penelope Reverse

THE DAWN OF TOURISM
1716 - 1788

After the destruction by Louis XIV of the fortress of Nice, the Comté, in a pacified context, reinforced its infrastructures (new port of Nice, carriage road to the Col de Tende) while there emerged a new activity, tourism.

An open city since the demolition of its castle, Nice had relinquished its key military role as illustrated in an episode of the War of Austrian Succession when the Gallispans (French and Spanish troops) easily took over the city in 1744, then after a Sardinian counter-offensive in 1746 retook it just as easily in 1747 before it was returned once again to Sardinia by the Treaty of Aix-la-Chapelle in 1749. After the reconciliation of France and Austria, the context of political appeasement made it possible, with the Treaty of Turin of 1760, to reach an agreement to settle the western border of the Comté de Nice on the Estéron and Var Rivers through an exchange of communes. This was done without consulting the people and the castle of Guillaumes was dismantled by the French before its transfer to Sardinia. Benefiting from this peaceful period, the Comté de Nice pursued its development. A new port, *Port Lympia*, was excavated east of the Castle Hill between 1750 and 1756. To improve connections with Turin, Victor Amedeus III (1773-1796) undertook titanic works to open the road to carriages from Nice to Turin over the Col de Tende between 1780 and 1788. The Comté de Nice remained nonetheless very poor and in the

Portrait of the Scotsman Tobias Smollett

Presumed portrait of Fragonard (Musée des beaux-arts et d'archéologie, Besançon).

mid-18th century had only 70,000 inhabitants, one-fourth in Nice. With tourism came economic prosperity. In 1763, the work published by the Scotsman Tobias Smollett, then the visit by the Duke of York, brother of the King in 1764, marked the beginning of the popularity of Nice with the British. Winter tourism brought over 300 foreigners in 1785 and gradually a new district of foreign homes arose to the west of Nice. The region of Grasse produced two famous figures: Jean-Honoré Fragonard, one of the finest French 18th-century painters, and Admiral de Grasse, a hero of the American Revolution.

Map of the Var département, created in 1790
(Archives départementales)

THE FRENCH REVOLUTION
1789 - 1791

The French Revolution, which divided France into départements in 1790, made Grasse and Saint-Paul district capitals dependent on Toulon, but Grasse and Vence lost their bishop's see. Unrest and the proximity of the border facilitated the émigrés' flight to Nice.

In July 1788, Louis XVI decided to convene the Estates-General to try to solve the kingdom's many problems, in particular the serious financial and economic crisis shaking the country. Clergy, aristocracy and the third estate each elected their representatives and drew up registers of grievances at the beginning of 1789. The main concerns of the people of Provence concerned seigniorial rights, the tithe, taxation, justice and the Provençal Constitution. The Seneschalsy of Grasse elected Mougins de Roquefort, a lawyer from Grasse, to represent the third estate. On May 5, the Estates-General met in Paris then became the Constituent Assembly. On July 14 the people stormed the Bastille, marking the onset of the Revolution. Provence experienced serious problems of subsistence after a very harsh winter and the region of Grasse was not spared by the threat of bands of looters. As soon as the suppression of privileges was announced on the night of August 4, the effervescence reached some communes hostile to their lords, like Vence, and émigrés began crossing into the Comté de Nice in the autumn. In February 1790, the new administrative organisation of France was set up: Toulon became the

Portrait of Mougins de Roquefort, mayor of Grasse, deputy of the Assembly of 1789
(Archives départementales)

prefecture of the Var département with nine districts including Grasse and Saint-Paul du Var. In July 1790, the adoption of the Civil Constitution of the Clergy led to the disappearance of the bishoprics of Grasse and Vence and a break between "constitutional" priests and "refractories". The religious question stirred unrest. In 1792, the problems worsened: in February rioters burned down the castle of Le Bar. Growing numbers of popular societies emphasised the repressive measures. Émigrés, aristocrats and clergy crowded into Nice as tension grew along the border.

Painting by Comba showing Bonaparte at the head of the French Army of Italy when he came to Nice in 1796 (Musée Masséna)

When the King of Sardinia declared war on France, Nice was quickly taken in September 1792. The Comté became the 85th département of France in February 1793. After the military upsets of 1793, General Masséna completed the conquest in 1794 but the Barbets' resistance persisted in the hinterland.

THE COMTÉ DE NICE IN REVOLUTIONARY HANDS
1792 - 1799

With his close family ties to the Bourbon dynasty and concerned by the threat of revolutionary contagion, Victor Amedeus III declared war on Revolutionary France on September 22, 1792. Savoy put up no resistance and the retreat of the troops in the Comté de Nice ordered by Turin enabled General d'Anselme's soldiers to enter Nice without difficulty, while many civilians and émigrés followed the routed Sardinian army out of Nice. A provisional administration was set up. On January 31, 1793, the Convention voted to annex the Comté, which became the 85th French département, which included the Principality of Monaco added ten days later. French representatives, including Abbé Grégoire, were sent to help organise it. But the war continued in 1793 with a Sardinian counteroffensive stopped with the Battle of Gilette by General Dugommier. In spring 1794, General Masséna reversed the situation. Although the French had complete control of the Comté in May 1794, there was continued resistance, with *coups de main* and harassment by the *Barbets* in the hinterland. Bonaparte came to Nice in 1796 for the Italian campaign, which further marked the Sardinian ruler's defeat. Victor Amedeus III

Portrait of General Masséna (Archives départementales)

ceded the Comté de Nice with the Treaty of Paris on May 15, 1796. But revolutionary ideas had little hold in the new département and many measures, such as "dechristianisation", were applied with caution for fear of exacerbating the people's hostility. Military requisitions for billeting and supplying troops weighed heavily on the population, however.

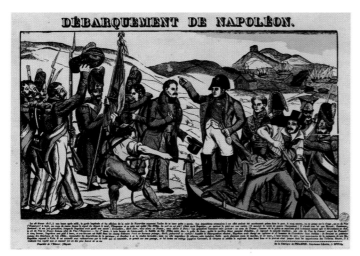

Napoleon I landing in Golfe-Juan on March 1, 1815.

The Empire established French institutions in the Alpes-Maritimes département and brought back stability, but the cost of France's European wars weighed increasingly on the local population, affected by economic troubles and resistance to military conscription.

THE SETBACKS OF THE EMPIRE
1800 - 1814

After the troubled Revolutionary years, the Empire brought pacification and stability with the reinforced power of the State in appointing a prefect and the General Council. The Prefect Dubouchage administered the département adroitly from 1804 to 1814 in spite of the difficulties due to resistance to taxation and especially the growing hostility to military conscription which gave rise to more and more insubordination. The efforts to improve sanitary conditions through vaccination, education (and Gallicisation with the new Lycée in 1812), transportation (in particular with the construction of the Grande Corniche road) and economic activity remained limited or were implemented only belatedly. Even though the département expanded with the annexation of the *arrondissement* of San Remo by decree of June 6, 1805, the precarious economy and limited resources made it fragile and with the population always at the mercy of climatic fluctuations. In 1812, bad harvests led to serious famine with its cortège of misery and begging. Maritime trade was hindered by privateering, in which Bavastro of Nice distinguished himself but the English stranglehold disrupted traffic. With Napoleon's abdication

Decree appointing the first members of the General Council of the Alpes-Maritimes, Year VIII (1800) (Archives départementales)

in April 1814, the prefect tried in vain to rally the Alpes-Maritimes to the new French King Louis XVIII. Gallicisation was superficial and the Comté de Nice returned to the Kingdom of Sardinia, marking the end of the first Alpes-Maritimes département. Napoleon's landing in Golfe-Juan in 1815 brought no political changes.

VUE DE LA CROIX DE MARBRE ET DE LA COLONNE ÉLEVÉE À PIE VII. À NICE.

La Croix-de-Marbre district in Nice in 1835 (Musée Massena)

In 1814 the Comté de Nice was restored to the Kingdom of Sardinia with all its institutions, but the monarchies were shaken by the liberal reaction. Another revolution re-established the Republic in France in 1848 while Menton and Roquebrune rebelled against the Prince of Monaco. In the face of this revolutionary surge, the King of Sardinia was forced to have a new constitution drawn up reducing his powers: the Statuto.

RESTORATION AND REVOLUTIONS
1814 - 1851

The Restoration marked the return of royalty for both the *arrondissement* of Grasse and the Comté de Nice, which returned to Sardinian King Victor-Emmanuel I. The *ancien régime* was restored in all its aspects: institutions (the Senate, in particular), the role of the Church (suppression of the registry office, replacement of the Imperial Lycée by the Jesuit school). The first liberal reaction broke out in Turin in 1821 but failed and Saluzzo, Governor of Nice, easily contained the movement. In July 1830, Revolution shook up the regime in France. Economic development remained modest in the Comté in spite of the expansion of tourism with the return of the English. The *arrondissement* of Grasse also benefited from this trend, especially Cannes when Lord Brougham was forced to stop there after being unable to cross the border closed off by quarantine set up by the Sardinian authorities as protection against a cholera epidemic. The arrondissement of Grasse also enjoyed sustained economic activity thanks to the development of the perfume industry. Intellectual and artistic life prospered in Nice with the poet Rancher, the painters Trachel and Fricero and the naturalist Risso, but the city lost its medical and law schools to Turin

Portraits of the brothers Auguste and Adolphe Blanqui (Archives départementales)

in 1844 and 1848. In 1832, the *Consiglio d'Ornato* ensured harmonious urban planning in Nice (with the construction of Place Massena starting in 1835 and the Port in 1840). After repressing the liberals in 1833 and quelling the uprising led in 1834 by Garibaldi, who was born in Nice and fled to South America, King Charles Albert (1831-1849), like other absolute monarchs, was confronted with the revolutionary surge that shook Europe in 1848. On March 4, 1848, he proclaimed the *Statuto*, which brought a profound change in the regime and reduced the King's power by instituting two assemblies. The impasse of the war with Austria in 1849 led Charles Albert to abdicate in favour of his son. Also in 1848, Menton and Roquebrune were able to free themselves totally from Monegasque control by placing themselves under Sardinian protection. Even more radical, the revolution in France reinstated the Republic, but the conservatives limited the most extremist movements, including that of the socialist theoretician Louis Auguste Blanqui, born in Puget-Théniers. Louis Napoleon Bonaparte was elected President of the Republic in December 1848.

Engraving showing the arrival of the French representatives
to take over the arrondissement of Nice in 1860
(Archives départementales)

In 1852 the reaction against Napoleon's coup d'état
was particularly strong in Provence where it was
repressed. The Empire was restored. In the Province of
Nice, the suppression of the free port and the now
preponderant role of Genoa favoured the emergence of
a pro-French party. Napoleon III's support of the King of
Sardinia's policy towards Italian unity enabled him to
annex Nice and Savoy in 1860. A new Alpes-Maritimes
département was created to which was added the
arrondissement of Grasse.

THE RETURN OF THE EMPIRE
1852 - 1860

Cavour's liberal free-exchange policy led to a customs reform that, in spite of the very strong opposition of the people of Nice, became effective in 1853. Nice, which had become a minor port and declined after the annexation of Genoa to the Kingdom of Sardinia in 1815, received the *coup de grâce* with the suppression of its free port. When the Senate lost its administrative status, the pro-French party began making headway in economic circles at a time when the Comté was stagnating, while neighbouring France seemed to be in full expansion. Avigdor founded a French-language paper, *L'écho des Alpes-Maritimes*, militating for annexation. In 1852, Louis Napoleon's coup d'état restored the Empire and triggered a large-scale uprising in Provence, but the supporters of the Republic were crushed. Some, like Alphonse Karr, who fled the coup d'état, reinforced the pro-French party in Nice. To defend the interests of their foreign policy devoted to establishing Italian unification, Victor Emmanuel II and Cavour pursued their sacrifice of the Comté de Nice after the secret agreement of January 1859 with Napoleon III, intended to secure a powerful ally against Austria. Cavour's provocations quickly led to war, where

Portrait of Tsarina Alexandra
(Painting by Fricero)

Garibaldi distinguished himself. The Franco-Sardinian troops vanquished the Austrian army at Solferino on June 24. In spite of the French disengagement in exchange for recognition of Italian unity, Victor Emmanuel II gave his approval for the transfer of Savoy and Nice on condition of the consent of their population. Everything was combined for their acceptance. The plebiscite was held on April 15, 1860, under careful supervision of the French and Sardinian civil and religious authorities. The result was as expected: 99% of the electors chose annexation to France, which became effective on June 14, 1860. But the new Alpes-Maritimes département was not the same as during the French Revolution. It gained the *arrondissement* of Grasse detached from the Var, but ceded Tende, La Brigue and territories enabling Italy to control the mountain passes. It did, however, include the communes of Menton and Roquebrune, in exchange for financial compensation to Monaco.

Poster of the international exhibition at Le Piol in 1884 (Archives départementales)

THE RAILWAY
1861 - 1886

The Empire's large investments in the Alpes-Maritimes ensured the département's economic development. The arrival of the railway in Nice in particular was an essential factor for the growth of tourism and the development of horticulture. The fall of the Second Empire in 1870 in no way called into question the allegiance of Nice to France in spite of the emergence of an ephemeral separatist party.

The first decade of the Alpes-Maritimes was characterised by unprecedented investments. The railway reached Nice in 1864 and Menton in 1869. The east bank of the Var River was dyked up over the entire lower course. Large-scale road works were undertaken, in particular the Road along the Lower Var Valley and the Basse Corniche to open up the département. The railway favoured the development of horticulture and fresh-cut flowers (the carnation of Nice and mimosa).

In 1870, after the defeat of Sedan, Léon Gambetta, whose family was from Nice, contributed to re-establishing the Republic and distinguished himself in the country's defence. The defeat of 1870 and the fall of the Empire favoured the emergence of a separatist party in Nice that managed to win the municipal elections. Those ideas were expressed by the newspaper *Il Pensiero di Nizza* that began publication in 1871. But the movement was short-lived, and supporters of the Republic in favour of greater integration, like Alfred Borriglione, won out in the end.

The activity in the Port of Nice gradually increased. In 1880 a new breakwater was built and an outer harbour was created in

The new railway station in Nice in 1865 (Archives départementales)

1890. Cannes, Antibes, Nice and Menton exported foodstuffs (olive oil, wine, citrus fruit) and merchandise (wood, bricks, pottery, etc.) throughout the Mediterranean as well as Great Britain, Scandinavia and Russia.

The farming of plants for perfumery was closely linked to the development of the industry in Grasse and the technical advances made in the late 19th century with the industrial application of the extraction process for perfume with volatile solvents by Chiris. The expansion of perfumery was accompanied by the creation of many plants: Lautier, Roure, Mero, Tombarel, Giraud, etc. Other industries arose and modernised: soap makers, flour mills, glassworks in La Bocca, a cork factory in Mandelieu, the tobacco factory in Nice, copper mining... The département's economic upswing was materialised in the 1884 international exhibition, where electricity made its first appearance in Nice.

Watercolour by Mossa showing the first automobile race from Marseille to Nice on Promenade des Anglais in 1897 (Musée Massena)

The Belle Époque was a time of radical change in the département. While the Riviera, newly dubbed Côte d'Azur by Stephen Liégeard, was covered with luxury hotels and sumptuous homes, the hinterland was deserted because of rural exodus and the decline of traditional activities.

THE "CÔTE D'AZUR"
1887 - 1913

As rural exodus began to have serious consequences in the hinterland where mountain farming declined, there was profound demographic upheaval on the Coast. From less than 50,000 inhabitants at the time of annexation to France, the population of Nice rose to 142,000 at the 1911 census. Tourism considerably influenced urban development both in Nice with the extension of Promenade des Anglais and in Cannes with the construction of La Croisette. This was the period of urbanisation of the district of Cimiez, with the construction of sumptuous hotels like the Regina (1896) and the Negresco (1913) in Nice or the Carlton in Cannes (1912) and of prestigious casinos, like the *Jetée Promenade* in Nice. Electricity became widespread in 1893 in Nice and, in 1896, *la Société des forces motrices des Alpes-Maritimes* built the first waterfall on the Var River at La Mescla gorges. Every winter, the French Riviera, dubbed Côte d'Azur in 1887 by Stephen Liégeard, became the privileged residence of the European élite: Queen Victoria came every year from 1895 to 1899; her Prime Minister, Lord Salisbury, had an estate in Beaulieu; the King of Belgium settled on Cap Ferrat; the King of Sweden went to

The Russian orthodox cathedral built with the help of Tsar Nicholas II

The Hôtel Negresco built in a pastiche of the 18th-century architectural style with its cupola designed by Gustave Eiffel.

Cannes; the Russian aristocracy and the Imperial family gathered in Cannes, Nice and Menton. It was for this large community that the magnificent Russian cathedral was built, with support from Tsar Nicholas II. More and more artists and writers flocked here: the writers Guy de Maupassant, Antoine Chekhov and Friedrich Nietzsche, the composer Jules Massenet, the painters Claude Monet and Auguste Renoir who settled in Cagnes in 1903.

Tourism was accompanied by brilliant social life, athletic events (regattas, golf after 1892, tennis) and festivities: flower processions and especially the Carnival of Nice, restructured in 1873, whose renown spread after 1882, when the painter Mossa designed the first float for King Carnival.

The automobile revolutionised transport after its appearance on the Riviera in 1893 and one of the oldest races, the La Turbie hill climb, was held in 1897.

Notes printed by the Chamber of Commerce in 1920 (Archives départementales)

The département was not spared by the First World War, in spite of its distance from the front. Refugees and wounded soldiers were housed in requisitioned hotels and the département experienced major economic problems and suffered loss of human lives.

WORLD WAR I
1914 - 1918

The main activity in the Alpes-Maritimes, tourism, was severely shaken by the War, which broke out on the eve of the winter season in 1914. It marked the end of the Belle Époque. After losing much of their clientele, many hotels were requisitioned to accommodate the wounded brought in at the beginning of the war because of fierce combat and its many fatalities. In December 1914, the Alpes-Maritimes had nearly 12,000 beds for the wounded and convalescent thanks to the conversion of several luxury hotels into hospitals. Many civilian refugees, up to 11,000 in September 1918, came in from the regions invaded or located in the combat zone. Their situation was precarious in spite of assistance, because of the département's growing economic problems. Farming production, affected by the lack of labour due to mobilisation, no longer covered local needs and the transport crisis at the end of 1917 only aggravated the situation. Requisitions and restrictions were imposed in an unprecedented war effort to ensure armament and supply of troops and equipment. For the first time women played a determinant role in economic activity, replacing male workers. Shortages and rising prices were accompanied by a monetary

Sick ward in Hôtel Royal in Nice, requisitioned in 1915 (Archives départementales)

crisis requiring the issuance of tokens and small notes by the Chambers of Commerce starting in 1918. To fund the war, the government raised taxes, instituted income tax in 1916, launched loans calling on the patriotism of the French people. Solidarity with the fighting men and orphans was manifest with days devoted to collection for charity and raffles, too often repeated to maintain the donors' spirit of giving, as well as charity performances, that became the only surviving form of entertainment. Although spared by the unprecedented destruction of war, the Alpes-Maritimes département bore the scars of tremendous loss of life, with over 9,000 dead, and the lasting consequences of such imbalance. The trauma was expressed in a new holiday, on November 11, and the construction of war memorials, the one in Nice being inaugurated by Marshal Foch in 1928.

Advertisement for coach service, cars de haute Tinée (Archives départementales).

Manager of the service station in Saint-Laurent-du-Var, 1928 (Archives départementales)

In spite of the problems resulting from the war, the French Riviera soon renewed with its activity, increased by the beginnings of summer tourism. This was the glorious time of the Roaring Twenties, with the rise of cinema and the birth of radio

THE ROARING TWENTIES
1919 - 1929

Although France was in a disastrous situation after the War, with inflation growing faster than salaries (a source of social unrest), the French Riviera soon enjoyed economic expansion thanks to tourism, with renewed activity and especially a new trend: summer visitors. By 1921, thanks to the American Frank Jay Gould, Juan-les-Pins became a renowned summer resort where women discovered the joys of tanning, made fashionable by Coco Chanel. The extraordinary prosperity in the post-war years and the fever of speculation that took over the Riviera brought in massive numbers of foreigners, most from Italy and Russia, too, so much so that in 1926 they represented nearly one-third of the population in the département. In Nice, *Le Palais de la Méditerranée*, inaugurated in 1929, symbolised this prosperous era. This vast luxury recreational complex, designed by the architects Charles and Marcel Dalmas, illustrated the modernity that revolutionised building methods. The French Riviera became one of the privileged venues where new artistic trends were expressed. It was in Nice that Matisse executed in 1920 his admirable series of Odalisques while Picabia set himself up as a precursor of the Surrealist

The first radio station on the French Riviera set up in Juan-les-Pins (Archives départementales)

Matisse on his boat in Nice, 1929 (Archives départementales)

movement in painting.

In the area of leisure activities, the Riviera renewed with the splendour of its festivities, the most striking phenomenon was the popular success of talking pictures after 1928 and the appearance of the radio. The first radio station in south-eastern France, *Radio LL*, was set up in 1927 in Juan-les-Pins. The French Riviera became a major film centre with the creation of studios, including La Victorine in 1919, where Rex Ingram shot many films.

In the area of sporting events, the automobile enjoyed growing popularity with many rally races and formula races including the Grand Prix of Monaco first run in 1929.

Shopkeepers' pamphlet against the opening of Prisunic stores, 1933 (Archives départementales)

Employers' poster against the 40-hour workweek, c. 1935 (Archives départementales)

The economic crisis of 1930 had strong repercussions on tourism. The big hotels were on the brink of bankruptcy and other economic activities were affected in turn; unemployment was rampant. In spite of extreme rightwing propaganda, the département elected two Communist deputies to join the Popular Front in 1936. Tensions with Fascist Italy worsened in the département with its large immigrant community.

THE TROUBLED YEARS
1930 - 1939

After the crash on the New York Stock Exchange in October 1929, the Depression hit the French Riviera very early, since its tourist activity made it very dependent on the international economy. In 1933 there were 57% fewer tourists; bankruptcy was everywhere; 35 big hotels closed between 1930 and 1937 including the Majestic and the Regina in Nice.

All activity sectors were concerned: industry, perfumery, commerce, which was changing with the appearance in 1933 of large popular *Prisunic* stores, and farming, already hard hit by the decline in traditional production. The limitation of exports of perfumes caused a collapse in the price of flowers (with the total value of production dropping from 65 to 3 million French francs from 1928 to 1932).

Unemployment spread despite measures to cut down on foreign labour and the organisation of major public works projects. The incapacity of governments to solve the crisis and corruption fuelled antiparliamentary attitudes and rightwing unrest gave rise to active campaigning in the Alpes-Maritimes. In the face of the extremist threat and the rise of fascism, with Italian socialists seeking refuge in the Alpes-Maritimes, the leftwing

Virgile Barel in Breil for the victory of the Popular Front, 1936 (Archives départementales)

parties joined forces to give victory to the Popular Front in the elections of 1936.

For the first time, the département sent two Communist deputies, Virgile Barel and Henri Pourtalet, to the National Assembly. In spite of measures like paid holidays that changed the patterns of tourism on the Riviera, the economic crisis persisted and political unrest was exacerbated. Anti-Semitism, latent since the Dreyfus affair, now came out in the open with increasing verbal violence to the point of inciting to murder. The inexorable crisis with Germany led to the explosion of the Popular Front. On August 23, 1939, the signature of the Soviet Pact with Hitler provided an opportunity for anticommunist repression. With the invasion of Poland on September 1, 1939, Britain and France declared war on Hitler, while Mussolini's alliance with Germany represented a direct threat to the Alpes-Maritimes.

Mussolini and Marshal Badoglio reviewing the Italian occupation troops in Menton, 1941 (Archives départementales)

After the defeat of France in 1940, the département was occupied first by the Italians, then the Germans in 1943. Repression increased against the Jews as well as against the Resistance. Following the Allied landing on August 15, 1944, the département was soon liberated, but the Germans resisted in l'Authion massif until April 1945. The intervention of the First Free French Division led to the annexation of Tende and La Brigue to France.

THE WAR YEARS
1940 - 1945

After the military disaster of May 1940 and the signature of the armistice of June 22, 1940, France was cut in two and largely occupied by the Germans. In the Alpes-Maritimes the communes of Menton and Fontan were annexed *de facto* by Italy. With his headquarters in Vichy, Marshal Pétain was invested with full powers and instituted a dictatorship, the National Revolution. Pétain was very popular in the Alpes-Maritimes, where he had a home in Villeneuve-Loubet. The success of mass demonstrations of 1941 earned Nice the nickname "eldest daughter of the National Revolution". But gradually the cleansing, repression, growing collaboration with the Germans after April 1942 and roundups of Jews in August 1942 by the French authorities in the Alpes-Maritimes led to the emergence of Resistance movements. It was especially the conscription of French workers instituted in February 1943 that encouraged dissidents to form the first Maquis. After a period devoted essentially to propaganda through the underground press and pamphlets, the Resistance, armed by parachuting operations starting in 1943, began attacking the occupation forces and collaborators directly through executions, attacks and sabotage.

De Gaulle in Nice, April 9, 1945 (Archives départementales)

Tank in Cannes after the liberation, August 1944 (Archives départementales)

But the fall of Mussolini led to the occupation of the Alpes-Maritimes in September 1943 by the Germans, who reinforced repression and undertook titanic fortification works along the coast. The Germans practised merciless repression against members of the Resistance, with summary executions in 1944 of secondary school students of the Lycée Massena at Saint-Julien-du-Verdon, the hanging of Torrin and Grassi in Nice, etc. The first large-scale action of the Resistance was triggered by the ORA on July 7, 1944, in the upper Var Valley. The Allied landing in Provence on August 15, 1944, was the signal of a general offensive. As American troops progressed quickly on the west bank of the Var, an insurrection in Nice on August 28 forced the Germans to retreat, but at the end of the year, they still held a fortified line in l'Authion massif. General de Gaulle came to Nice on April 9, 1945, and engaged the First Free French Division to complete liberation of the territory. The victorious French offensive led to the annexation of Tende and La Brigue, ratified by popular vote.

The Riviera International Airport, 1963 (photograph: lab. dép. de l'équipement, Archives départementales)

The reconstruction after World War II gave the Alpes-Maritimes département new infrastructures (airport, motorway) that contributed to unprecedented prosperity and uncontrolled urban growth along the coast, while the rural exodus in the hinterland was slowed by the development of winter resorts.

RECONSTRUCTION
1946 - 1970

The region recovered with difficulty from the damage accumulated during the war: summer tourism, which had now become predominant, was slow in starting off again, due to the presence of German landmines along the access to the beaches. The first International Film Festival in 1946 asserted the prestige of Cannes. The re-establishment of major communication systems, but especially their development with the rapid growth of the airport of Nice first opened in 1946 and construction of the first motorway in 1961, paved the way to unprecedented economic prosperity.

Popular tourism became preponderant with the improved standard of living. More and more yachting harbours were developed on the Coast, after Port Canto in Cannes in 1964. Winter tourism gave the hinterland a boost with the construction of huge recreational real estate projects in the ski resorts. The latest such resort, Isola 2000, opened in 1971. The Alpes-Maritimes, with no industrial tradition except perfumery in Grasse, became a region of state-of-the-art technology opening onto outside markets. In the early 1960s, large multinational companies in the sectors of electronics and information technology established themselves here:

Works on the motorway through the Alpes-Maritimes in 1961 (photograph: lab. dép. de l'équipement, Archives départementales)

Texas Instrument in Villeneuve-Loubet in 1961, the IBM European Research Centre in La Gaude in 1962, while the aeronautics company in Cannes, successor to the aeroplane maker Romano, participated in French and European satellite construction programmes after 1965.

The university founded in Nice in 1965 developed many research laboratories.

The strong demographic growth (approximately 100,000 more inhabitants with each census since 1954) ensured by regular immigration (repatriated settlers from Algeria in particular) led to mediocre uncontrolled urban expansion that spoiled the coast.

Picasso, Chagall, Léger and Nicolas de Staël contributed to the French Riviera's reputation as a Mecca for contemporary art, confirmed with the construction of the Maeght Foundation.

Built in a forest of Aleppo pine and live oak, the Sophia Antipolis Science and Technology Park covers 2,400 ha between Antibes and Valbonne and houses companies using advanced technology, educational institutions and research organisations.

At the end of the 20th century, the activity of the Alpes-Maritimes département is no longer oriented essentially on tourism. The location of cutting-edge enterprises in the areas of electronics and telecommunications around the Science and Technology Park of Sophia Antipolis has provided a new industrial vocation. In spite of its economic weight, Nice was not able to obtain the regional power legitimised by Europe.

ECONOMIC PROSPERITY
AND INSTITUTIONAL WEAKNESS
1971 - 1990

There occurred a change in the conditions of tourism in the 1970s. The frequent organisation of conventions helped provide its numerous clientele with the specific facilities they demanded. The airport contributed in large part to the success of such tourism and its traffic. The largest provincial airport in France, it continued growing to reach 6 million passengers. To respond to this clientele, the Mayor of Nice built an impressive complex in 1984, the Acropolis Convention Centre. In 1977 a gigantic construction site was opened to extend the airport on the sea and create a new port, but a ground swell carried off part of the fill in 1979.

Starting in 1970 an ambitious industrial policy takes shape. After the zone of Carros, there was the Sophia Antipolis Technology Park, based on a concept launched by Senator Laffitte in 1969, now the fifth largest such park worldwide. In 15 years some one hundred businesses located here, giving the Alpes-Maritimes département its first industrial dimension in the new technologies of electronics, computer science and telecommunications. With no existing dense industrial fabric, the département was spared the great crisis of industrial change that

The Festival Hall and Convention Centre of Cannes was built in 1982, on the site of the former municipal casino. Today it hosts the International Film Festival and many other events.

affected many regions. Nonetheless, after 1990 and the Gulf War, the real estate recession struck a severe blow to the key traditional construction and public works sector.

The Alpes-Maritimes département was now at the forefront in terms of economic potential and demographic growth, but remained penalised from an institutional standpoint because of the lack of major decision-making centres in a context where Europe is emphasising the weight of Regions. The dream of a Riviera Region, like the claim for a court of appeals, has failed so far, because of fierce opposition from some quarters.

ACKNOWLEDGEMENTS

We would like to express our gratitude to the following persons and institutions
for their help in completing this book, thanks to their work, advice and archives:

The General Council of the Alpes-Maritimes

CONSEIL GENERAL
DES ALPES-MARITIMES

who provided the necessary support
to make this book possible.

The Provence-Alpes-Côte d'Azur Regional Council

LA RÉGION

Jean-Bernard Lacroix,
Director, Archives départementales des Alpes-Maritimes
Marie-Laure Robinson,
Assistant Curator to the Director, Archives départementales des Alpes-Maritimes,
who developed and illustrated the chapter "Land of History".

Jean-Loup Fontana,
Curator of the Heritage of the département
Michel Graniou
Photographer
for their invaluable advice and photographic documents respectively
for "Land of Religion".

Jean-Paul Potron,
Librarian, Bibliothèque de Cessole,
for providing rare documents from
the Chevalier de Cessole's Library at the Musée Masséna in Nice.

Claude Raybaud
for the two splendid panoramas taken from the coast
and his participation in writing the captions for the chapter on the Mercantour Park.

All the Municipalities in the Alpes-Maritimes
who kindly provided documentation
to produce this book.

For more information on the Alpes-Maritimes département
Contact the *Comité Régional du Tourisme Riviéra Côte d'Azur* (CRT) - 55, Promenade des Anglais - 06000 Nice
Tel.: +33 (0)4 93 37 78 78 - fax: +33 (0)4 93 86 01 06
E-mail : crt06@nicematin.fr - Internet : http://www.crt-riviera.fr

Publisher	Editions Gilletta - Nice
Artistic design	Claude and Gilbert Grisoni
Graphic design - Studio	Grégoire Gardette Edition - Nice
Photoengraving	Megapom - Nice
Printing	Imprimix - Nice
Binding	S.I.R.C. - Marigny le Chatel

Photographs by
Richard Wacongne

other photographic credits:

Miguel Ajuria • Alcatel • Muriel Anssens • Yves Bérard • Bibliothèque de Cessole • J.C. Braconnot
Stéphane Brasca • Gérald Bremond • C.G.A.M. / Georges Véran • Henri Del Olmo • Yann Duvivier
Ecomusée du Pays de la Roudoule • Editions Gilletta / Claude et Gilbert Grisoni • François Fernandez
Patrick Gérin • Claude Germain • Bernard Giani • Miguel Giugno • N. Giusto Magnardi
Jacques Godard • G.Gorsky • Michel Graniou • Martin Gray • Béatrice Heyligers • Norbert Huffschmitt
Image du Sud / G. de Tonge • Image du Sud / N. Jaubert • Image du Sud / D. Martin • Image du Sud /le Studio
André Kertesz • Gregory Krisanaz • Vincent Kulesza • Etienne Leperlier • Serge Lido • Jean-Christophe Maury
Laurence Monneret • Office du Tourisme de Mougins • Principality of Monaco Tourist Bureau
Dominique Petry-Amiel • Musée Picasso • Philippe Poulailler • David Reekie • Diane Richard
Pierre Roche • Elisabeth Rossolin • Guy Rottier • Jacques Schlienger • SBM /Loli • SBM /Belzil
Jean-Pierre Soardi • Alain Rozenbaum • Horenne Tinel • Bernard Touillon • Emmanuel Valentin
Thierry Valfort • City of Cannes • City of Menton • City of Nice • André Villers
Virbac • Nicolas Vitasse • World Magazine • Dominique Zintzmeyer

Maps: Jean-François Ferrandez (all rights reserved)

First printed in January 1999
by IMPRIMIX, Nice

ISBN - 2-903574-26-X
© Les Editions GILLETTA, 5 rue Michel Ange 06100 Nice
Tel.: +33 (0)4 93 51 94 94 - Fax: +33 (0)4 93 52 55 04
E-mail : edgilletta@aol.com

Map of the Alpes-Maritimes département - Côte d'Azur (French Riviera) - France